Until My Blindfold Comes Off

A Journey of Vision without Sight

For we walk by faith, not by sight.
2 Corinthians 5:7 NKJV

Christopher H. Harvey

Copyright © 2008 by Christopher H. Harvey

Until My Blindfold Comes Off
A Journey of Vision without Sight
by Christopher H. Harvey

Printed in the United States of America

ISBN 978-1-60647-909-4

All rights reserved solely by the author. The author guarantees all contents are original and do not infringe upon the legal rights of any other person or work. No part of this book may be reproduced in any form without the permission of the author. The views expressed in this book are not necessarily those of the publisher.

Unless otherwise indicated, Bible quotations are taken from The HOLY BIBLE, NEW INTERNATIONAL VERSION®. Copyright © 1973, 1978, 1984 by International Bible Society. Used by permission of Zondervan.

Other Scripture quotations are from:

The Message. Copyright © 1993, 1994, 1995, 1996, 2000, 2001, 2002. Used by permission of NavPress Publishing Group.

Scripture quotations marked NLT are taken from The Holy Bible, New Living Translation, Copyright © 1996, 2004. Used by permission of Tyndale House Publishers, Inc., Wheaton, Illinois 60189. All rights reserved.

Scripture quotations marked NCV are taken from The New Century Version. Copyright © 2005 by Thomas Nelson, Inc. Used by permission. All rights reserved.

Scripture quotations marked NKJV are taken from The New King James Version. Copyright © 1982 by Thomas Nelson, Inc. Used by permission. All rights reserved.

www.xulonpress.com

Dedication

I dedicate *Until My Blindfold Comes Off* to those who have encouraged me so that I might be an encouragement to others.

To my parents, Howell and Lucille, and to my brother, Craig: You emotionally shared in my tragedy, and contributed to my recovery. Your continued support and love is invaluable to me to this day.

To my beautiful bride, Stephanie: You are my soul mate. You chose to marry me despite my disability, because our creator gave you a special heart. I thank God for you every day.

To my three children, Chad, Blake, and Tori: I am so proud of you—and each of you has enriched my life in a unique way. You had no choice in being raised by a blind dad. My prayer is that God will bless you immensely, in exchange for the burdens and shortcomings of life with a father who could not see.

To my other relatives, friends, colleagues, and clients: You have transported me, read to me, troubleshot my screenreader software for me, befriended me, been patient with me, color coordinated me, and helped me in many other ways. I want you to know something—each time you did such a thing for me, you actually did it unto Jesus.

Contents

Preface... ix
Part One: In the Face of Adversity............................... 11
  1. Into the Darkness 13
  2. Prepared by the Spirit... 23
  3. Ping-Pong Balls and Cupcake Tins....................... 27
  4. In Charlotte's Words: The Battle is Before Us...... 37
  5. Rally the Troops... 41
  6. In Craig's Words: Brothers in Arms..................... 45
  7. Choosing Forgiveness... 53
  8. Moving Forward 57
  9. The Victory Belongs to the Lord........................... 61
 10. Walking by Dog 69
 11. On My Own, But Not Alone 79
 12. Blazing the Brokerage Trail 83
 13. Soul Mate.. 91
 14. In Stephanie's Words: Blind Date 97
 15. Earthly Fatherhood—Playing it by Ear................ 101

Part Two: Reflections on a Life without Sight 117
   16. Stepping Onto the Stage 119
   17. Life with Four Senses 127
   18. Built for this World 139
   19. Picking Up Crosses Daily 149
   20. Phantom Vision and Light Deprivation 155
   21. Joy in All Circumstances 163
   22. The Fairness Trap 171
   23. Eternity Bound 179

Acknowledgments 189
A Note from the Author 191

Preface

For we walk by faith, not by sight.
2 Corinthians 5:7 NKJV

Adversity can strengthen or destroy a person. Although I lost my sight as a junior in college, I never lost my vision for leading a productive life. I have written about my journey as a blind man in the hope that you might find inspiration to achieve the unimaginable in your own life. My goal is to glorify our Creator and our risen Savior with the contents of this work.

In the book of John, Jesus and the disciples come across a blind man:

As he went along, he saw a man blind from birth. His disciples asked him, "Rabbi, who sinned, this man or his parents, that he was born blind?"

"Neither this man nor his parents sinned," said Jesus, "but this happened so that the work of God might be displayed in his life." John 9:1-3

It is in this spirit and with great humility that I have written about what God has done in and through me since I lost my sight in 1980. My greatest desire is to inspire you to be all you can be by relying on God and applying your talents to the circumstances of your life—no matter what you face. Let me share how God used adversity to strengthen me, and to help me become who he created me to be.

Starting with the night I was blinded, I invite you to come with me and see what it means to live my earthly life without sight. I give all the glory to God for who I am and what he has done with my blindness. Until I take my final breath, I will keep walking by faith and not by sight, because when I get to heaven, *my blindfold comes off foreve*r!

Part One:

In the Face of Adversity

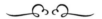

1

Into the Darkness

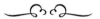

*For you intended to harm me, but God intended it
for good to accomplish what is now being done,
the saving of many lives.*
Genesis 50:20

*T*uesday, May 6, 1980. A series of loud pops broke the midnight calm as I paused from studying for my final exams to talk to my roommate, Hutch. My mind raced to identify the noise that sounded like gunfire outside our house. Two more pops filled the air, followed by metallic clanks.

The wall to my left exploded, but the room seemed to freeze into a snapshot. I sat motionless, the thudding of my heart pulsing in my ears as splinters of wood and insulation spewed into the room. The freeze-frame broke as a bullet pierced my skull and the impact spun me around and slammed me down onto the couch.

Hutched shouted, "Get down man!" as he dropped to the floor and scrambled on his belly to the wall-mounted phone in the parlor. The sound of the rotary dial played in my mind as my blood soaked the pillow on the couch. *This is crazy, I thought, I might be dying, and I'm preoccupied with the sound of the phone? Will it be the last sound I ever hear?*

The room began to spin and I felt like I was passing out. I told myself that I had to stay conscious. Would there be more gunshots? Would the shooter kick in the front door? Was I going to die? What had I done to provoke anyone?

Panicking, I sat up and cried out to Hutch. "I know this is sick, man, but how much of my face is gone?"

"It's all there. You're all right, man, get back down!"

I fell back onto the couch. I tried to look around, but everything was dark—a stark, formless darkness. A chill swept over me. I could see nothing.

I told myself to remain calm, but blood trickled down my throat, choking me. As the blood flow increased, I gagged and spit repeatedly. I was choking on my own blood, heaving, spitting, and gasping to pull air into my lungs. I heard the hollow sound of sirens and I relaxed a little, knowing help was nearly there.

***

Then a surreal feeling enveloped me. Some people refer to this feeling as an out-of-body experience but whatever it was, it occurred in the spiritual world. I seemed to retreat to some other realm and peered down into the living room. Although I could not see anything around me when I was on the couch, in this spiritual state I saw my rescuers at work. The body they attended to was mine, but I was separate from it. My spirit watched from above as one of the paramedics pulled the coffee table out of the living room and flung the rocking chair aside to clear the way to the couch. He wore a gray firefighter's jacket with tight elastic cloth cuffs, collar, and waistband. The other wore a navy blue flannel shirt with black buttons. As I watched the scene from above, I felt peaceful, as if I had been swept into the arms of the Holy Spirit. I did not want to leave the presence that surrounded me. I continued to look on as someone wheeled a gurney across the room. At that instant, my vantage point disappeared and I was again in the sightless body on the couch.

I made some silly attempt at control and started to get up to climb onto the gurney nearby. The deep voice of a paramedic warned, "Easy, now. We're here to help you. Lie back down and take it easy." He dabbed at my face with gauze, and then his fingers moved across my brow and into my hairline. "My buddy here is going to cut off your shirt. We need you to relax."

"My shirt?" It didn't matter at that point, and I acknowledged, "Okay."

"You need an IV. Easy now. You'll be all right." His voice reassured me, and I settled back, trying to stay calm while they did their job.

My awareness faded again, and my spirit returned to its peaceful viewpoint from above. I watched as two men approached the couch and lifted the body—my body—and strapped it onto the gurney. As much as I wanted to stay in the arms of God, my spirit re-entered my mortal body. I regained awareness from that viewpoint as the paramedics wheeled the gurney across the porch and handed me down the stairs to the waiting ambulance.

The local townies evidently huddled around to gawk, but their chatter faded as my stretcher passed them. The ambulance pulled away from the house and I slipped in and out of consciousness as we sped along the rural highway to Washington Hospital Center in Hagerstown, Maryland. I was faintly aware of the paramedics working on me. Their voices seemed distant as they discussed the obvious entry wound. They were uncertain of the exit location, or if the bullet remained in my head. Everything stayed pitch black and the reality of blindness began to take hold in my mind.

***

As I awaited x-rays in the emergency room, I vomited from swallowing blood. The nurse holding my bucket turned her head and loudly discussed soap operas with another nurse across the room while I continued to heave. I ached to have my parents with me. Had they been notified? Were they on the way? Meanwhile, the nurses chatted on—as though I wasn't there. I felt like shouting, "Take care of me. I'm hurt!"

I tried to convince myself that I didn't need the nurses. But I did need someone, and the inattention of the nurses seemed heartless to me. Then I recalled the words of Jesus on the cross, as he asked the Father to forgive those who were hurting him: "Forgive them, Father, for they do not know what they are doing" (Luke 23:34). I knew that those words related to my situation and the nurses. I knew they had to endure a lot of gore in their jobs and grew immune to the horror of it to survive. I could not hold a grudge against them.

***

After what seemed like hours, an emergency room physician approached me. "What's your name, son? What day is it? How old are you?" Even in my weakened state, I realized that he was judging my coherency. I answered the questions quickly and accurately.

His conversation with me switched from friendly to clinical and detached. "Your x-rays show bone and bullet fragments in the area behind your eyes." He ran his fingers along the right side and back of my head, the same as the paramedics had done in the ambulance. He took my chin in one hand, tilted my head back, and clicked his penlight. "Can you see anything? Any light at all?"

I stared into the darkness and dreaded voicing my answer. "Nope. Nothing. Just darkness."

The doctor said, "I want to fly you to the Wilmer Eye Clinic at Johns Hopkins Hospital in Baltimore."

"Do my parents know?"

"They've been contacted. They'll meet you at Hopkins."

The only medical transport helicopter was down for repairs, so the flight medic strapped my stretcher inside a bubble on the landing skid of a Maryland State Police helicopter. Inside the coffin-like bubble, I thought of the M.A.S.H. helicopters with their incoming wounded.

The aircraft shuddered as it began to rise. The isolation I had felt in the emergency room couldn't compare to the total abandonment I felt during the first moments of the flight. Like a little boy I prayed, "Father, I haven't had my career yet, haven't met my wife and had children yet. I know it's up to you whether I live or die, but I don't feel like my time here on earth should be over yet. If I am only blind, I'll live with it. God, please don't let me die. I'll deal with being blind if I have to."

Peace engulfed me, and I became aware of another presence with me: God, the creator of the universe. I relaxed in his care, drifting in and out of consciousness, suspended between heaven and earth.

***

When a Maryland State Trooper knocked on their door at two o'clock a.m., my parents feared something had happened to my brother, Craig, who was away on an overnight high school field trip. They were stunned to hear the news that I'd been shot, and immediately left for Johns Hopkins Hospital, less than an hour from their home.

As soon as the emergency team wheeled me away from the helicopter, Mom and Dad burst through the hospital doors and ran to my side. Mom's hand trembled as she touched my cheek, then she bent down and kissed me. Dad grasped my shoulder and told me I was going to be okay.

Mom could not hold back her tears, though, when she told me that I was going into surgery to determine the extent of my injury. "Surgery?" Panic ran through me, I thought I only had an eye injury. Surgery would mean going into my skull. Maybe God wasn't going to answer my prayer. Maybe I had brain damage, or maybe I was going to die.

An orderly came over. "The surgeon is ready for you, Mr. Harvey. We're going for a little ride." Mom and Dad held my hands and walked alongside the gurney as the orderly pushed it down the hallway.

Outside the surgical suite, Mom kissed me again, and her tears fell to my face. Dad squeezed my hand. "We'll see you after surgery, buddy. We'll be right here for you."

***

When I awoke in the recovery room, a doctor was in the chair beside my bed. He introduced himself as Dr. Lawrence Hirst, chief surgeon in charge of the Wilmer Eye Clinic. "Your surgery went well, but you were shot with a powerful hunting rifle. A bullet fragment entered your skull just behind your left eye, and exited behind your right eye. Both of your optic nerve bundles were severed, but fortunately the bullet missed your brain."

Fortunately? I knew it was a miracle, not fortune. I knew that God had heard my prayer in the helicopter and was allowing me more time on earth, and maybe he would restore my sight. I stopped the doctor's monologue and asked, "So, did you repair the nerves? Or do I have to have another surgery for that?"

Dr. Hirst continued, "No one can repair optic nerves."

"What about something experimental at a research hospital?"

"I'd fly in surgeons from across the globe if that would help, but nothing can bring back your sight."

He cleared his throat. "The damage can't be fixed. I'm sorry, but even with what technology is on the horizon, you will be blind for the rest of your life."

I'd held onto the possibility that my sight could be restored, but Dr. Hirst's words had the finality of a courtroom verdict: *Blind. Blind for life.*

"But if my eyeballs weren't destroyed—"

"Without the optic nerves, they can't function. They'll discolor and atrophy over time. You can wear dark glasses to cover them, but eventually they'll need to be removed."

"Removed? I'd have empty eye-sockets?"

"No, for cosmetic purposes we'd replace them with artificial eyes. It's up to you, but I'd recommend that you go ahead and have them removed now to avoid future infections and other complications."

Dr. Hirst wanted me to talk this over with my parents, but I knew my answer. I would surrender my God-given eyes, and accept my life of blindness. I would walk by faith, if not by sight, because *God had already prepared me for this tragedy.*

2

Prepared by the Spirit

When I was a child, I talked like a child, I thought like a child, I reasoned like a child. When I became a man, I put childish ways behind me. Now we see but a poor reflection as in a mirror; then we shall see face to face. Now I know in part; then I shall know fully, even as I am fully known.
1 Corinthians 13:11-12

This sounds strange, but during my childhood, I had a recurring awareness that I would not lead a normal adult life. I remember a time at my grandmother's house when I was seven or eight years old and wanted to hang around the adults while my brother and cousins played in the basement. Even at that age, I felt a great urgency to hurry up and experience adult life. My persistence with being around the adults often led my grandmother to say to me, "I declare,

Honey-child, for such a young man, you sure want to grow up too fast.

Want to grow up too fast, want to grow up too fast. Grandmother's words came back to me in my hospital bed. I didn't really *want* to grow up fast; I *had* to grow up fast. It is hard to put words to the awareness that swept over me time after time. More than a desire, this need to be an adult was overwhelming.

With a child's perception, I knew the awareness had to do with God's plan for my life. I didn't understand it, and how could a child explain this to anyone? Sometimes the awareness pressed on me like a heavy woolen coat that I wanted to throw off my back.

As I got older, I found myself thinking less about God and more about my own desires and ambitions. My Type A personality drove me to be as good as I could be at everything I attempted. I didn't want only to play football in high school—I wanted to make the All-County team and help win the championship. I accomplished both of these goals and played on the golf, baseball, and lacrosse teams during my four years at Atholton High. Academics were also important to me, and I was named to the National Honor Society on the same day that I made the All-County team as defensive tackle. Of course, I also majored in dating and worked summers and weekends at various jobs. When I set out for college, I planned to get a business degree and decide a career from there. Occasionally the childhood feeling would surface amid my many activities, but I'd rationalize it as one of my character traits—a trait that spurred my zeal to be the best in everything I attempted.

In my junior year at Shepherd College, a similar feeling came over me when the chance for more independence came up. I wanted the adult lifestyle of living off campus, so the opportunity to move into a rental house in nearby Sharpsburg, Maryland seemed perfect. On moving day, I arrived at the house with my belongings piled high in the bed of a borrowed pick-up truck.

I opened the tailgate to unload my furniture and was overwhelmed with an unsettling impression. Reality seemed to bend slightly—as if my surroundings were out of kilter. There was an unseen danger, an eerie awareness beyond my understanding. Looking back to that incident, I realize that the hillside where my assailant would launch his attack was across the street to my right. I was standing in the path that the bullet would travel only six months later.

Was the impression on moving day a warning that would have changed my future if I had understood it? Or was it a grieving in the heavenly realm as I moved onto the stage that God had been preparing me for since childhood?

3

Ping-Pong Balls and Cupcake Tins

*I tell you the truth, unless you change
and become like little children,
you will never enter the kingdom of heaven.
Matthew 18:3*

I awoke in the early morning after my operation, groggy from medicated sleep. I knew I was in the hospital, and I listened for clues to figure out my surroundings. Squeaking wheels of carts or gurneys, the drone of voices, or an occasional laugh from the nurses' station drifted into the room from the far left corner, off the foot of my bed. The doorway had to be there. There were no sounds on either side of me—no breathing, or rustling of sheets, so I figured I must be in a private room.

My arm brushed the cool metal railing of the hospital bed. I ran my hand along the railing—it consisted of two bars that ended midway down the bed, with a cord for the call button looped over the top bar. I didn't need eyes to visualize the shiny metal next to the crisp white sheets.

Touching the railing sent my thoughts to another bed, another time. *When I was a toddler, Mom and Dad placed rails on my first real bed to keep me safe. In a way, I guess this railing is like God keeping me safe. I could have been killed or suffered brain damage. God, thanks for answering my prayer, thanks for allowing me to be only blinded.*

My musing stopped when an orderly delivered my breakfast. When he saw the bandages over my eyes, he offered to get a nurse to help me eat.

"No thanks, I want to do this on my own, but if you could help by sliding the tray table to me and taking the lids off, I'd appreciate it."

I'd located the wrapped utensils when a nurse bustled in and insisted that she feed me. A protest didn't seem likely to help, so I opened my mouth on cue. But, excruciating pain shot through my face when I tried to chew the soft food. "That's to be expected," the nurse explained. "The facial nerves to the teeth and gums were also bruised when your optic nerves were severed." After a few bites, I told her I wasn't hungry and I wanted to rest.

She left and I thought I'd be alone until my parents arrived mid-morning.

My solitude soon ended. "Good Morning, Chris. My name is Charlotte Gale Seltser. I'm the rehabilitation specialist here at Wilmer." Her cheerful voice radiated a hope that I hadn't heard from anyone else in the clinic. There were no platitudes and no pity as she talked to me about my surgery. I could sense she was all about the business of getting me back up on my feet, and knew exactly what it would take. Then she said, "I have something here I'd like to show you, if you're up to it."

Her tone intrigued and energized me. "Sure. I'm not very busy. Whatcha got?" She placed a metal object in my hand and asked if I knew what it was. I ran my hands across the object. "Feels like a small cupcake tin to me."

"That's right, a six-cup tin. And do you know what these are?" Charlotte pressed smooth, round items into my waiting hands.

"Ping-pong balls?"

"Right again. Now, are you ready to learn Braille?"

The reality of the first step to recovery consumed me. I quickly assessed there was no need to waste time, and answered, "Well yeah, why not?"

Charlotte explained that Braille consisted of cells with one to six raised dots. We would use the cupcake tin as the cell and the ping-pong balls as the dots. "Every Braille character, whether a letter, a symbol, or a number, is called a cell. Every cell is a combination of six possible raised dots."

She turned the cupcake tin to represent a three-up, two-across cell and placed my hands on it. "The top left dot, or cup in the tin, is number one. We go down the column for number two and number three. The top right is number four, with five and six below." Charlotte moved my fingers to feel each indentation as she spoke. "Got that? Or do you want me to go over it again?"

"I think I've got it. But maybe one more time would be good."

Charlotte repeated the code.

"Let me try now." I put a finger in the top left cup. "This is number one. Right beside it is number four." Then I moved down, "This is number two, here is three, back up to number four, and down to five and six."

Charlotte dropped a ball into cup one. "This represents the letter 'A.' The other positions in the cell are empty. In Braille, the raised dot would be in this position, with no other dots in the cell."

She dropped another ball into the second position. "Dots or balls in positions one and two represent the letter 'B.' See?" She placed my hands over the balls in the cupcake tin.

And on she went. We made it through the letter "J" before my strength drained. "Let's stop for now, I need to rest."

As Charlotte left the room, I heard a nurse snap, "Mrs. Seltser! I need to speak with you…now."

***

The next morning, two nurses came in to take me to the bathroom—my first trip out of the bed. One nurse lowered the rail and helped me to a sitting position. "Sit up right there for a minute. If you aren't feeling dizzy, we'll try to get you up. Do you think you can walk a few steps?"

"Of course I can. It's my eyes that aren't working, not my legs," I teased. "Move this guardrail and point me in the right direction."

After sitting upright for a minute or so, I swung my legs over the edge of the bed. With a nurse on either side of me, I gradually eased my weight onto my feet and stood. I wouldn't admit that I felt woozy, and I told the nurses I was ready to go. One hooked her arm under my left armpit, and the other slid my IV pole along on the right. I shuffled my feet across the floor in the direction they were guiding. Once inside the small cubicle, they placed my left hand on the sink, and then described the position of the commode to the left of the sink, and the tub next to the commode. The wooziness had subsided a little, so I defended my male pride and shooed them away.

"Thanks, ladies, but I can handle things from here." They were hesitant, but I insisted I was okay.

"We'll be right outside of the door, Mr. Harvey. You call out if you need us."

As soon as they heard a flush, the door flew back open.

"Here is the soap and a washcloth. And your toothbrush is right here, with toothpaste already on it." Talk about service. I'm sure I could have opened a tube of toothpaste by myself, but why not relax and be treated like a king of sorts for a while?

My escorts and I headed back to the bed, with me shuffling along between them. The fragrance of clean sheets engulfed me as I crossed the room, and I knew that the linens were changed while I was in the bathroom. The nurses helped me into bed and positioned the pillow behind my head. As I drifted off to sleep, I realized that after only two days without sight, I was already using my senses of touch, hearing, and smell to create a mental image of my surroundings. I savored the memory of faces and places, of shapes, colors, and depth perception—memories that would become a visual inventory to help me cope with blindness. And I thanked God for giving me twenty years with sight.

***

Later that day, Charlotte visited me. I demonstrated mastery of the letters she'd taught me and challenged her to test me. She arranged and rearranged the balls in the tin and I read them to her.

"Goodness, Chris, you've really been thinking about this since I was here yesterday."

"Hey, that's not all I've done since you were here." I almost felt like a child as I proudly reported that I'd walked to the bathroom with the nurses, and took care of business on my own.

"That's grand. You don't want to overdo it, but when you are ready to tackle more walking, let me know and I'll help you."

I piped up. "Now is good."

"Now?"

"Yes, now."

"I don't know, Chris. Are you sure?"

"Come on, Charlotte…"

"Okay, let me check to see how busy the hallways are."

She walked to the door, hesitated a moment, then came back to my bedside.

"There isn't too much traffic right now, let's go." She lowered the railing on my bed and helped me put on my slippers. "Let me know the second you don't feel like going any further, or if you feel at all dizzy, and we'll come right back. Now, hold your IV pole with your right hand, and grab my arm above my elbow."

So began my first lesson in walking without sight. Holding onto the IV pole with my right hand, and Charlotte with my left, I gently shuffled along, feeling my way across the room with my feet. Charlotte stopped before the doorway, took my hand from her arm, and placed it on the doorjamb.

"Here is the right side of the door. You want to miss it with the pole, so move a little to the left with me as we come through here."

A picture of the doorway popped into my mind as I touched the framework. Then, turning right into the hallway, I followed Charlotte's lead. I realized that we were turning right to avoid the nurses' station as a nurse shouted out to Charlotte from the left.

When Charlotte didn't answer, I muttered to her, "Are we in trouble?"

"Just keep walking." We inched down the hall, away from the nurses' station, with me pulling the IV pole right along.

"Listen to the voices and sounds as we walk. Think about the direction the sounds come from."

I was amazed that, without visual distractions, I could hear or sense changes in sound when we neared a wall or walked into an open area. My footsteps, the rolling wheels of the IV pole, and our voices echoed more when we were near a wall. Narrow halls enhanced the sounds, but open spaces caused them to dissipate.

Charlotte pointed out how the sound opened to our left when we came to a turn in the hall. "Do you hear the child's voice in front of us? Her voice is projecting away from us, right?"

Yes, I could tell that she was not walking toward us.

"We are walking faster than she is, and since her back is to us, we need to let her know we are here," Charlotte continued. "Why don't you warn them that we are approaching?"

I spoke up, "Excuse us, please," as we passed.

"Your hearing helps you visualize your surroundings. See?"

I did see. We turned and walked back toward my room.

As we neared the room, a nurse apprehended us. "Charlotte. What *are* you doing?"

I answered for Charlotte, "We're taking a walk."

"Well, you need to be resting, you've had major surgery.

Then she spoke again to Charlotte, "Do you have permission from Dr. Hirst?"

I interrupted again, "I'm okay. I asked to go for a walk."

We ended our walk that day, and I climbed back into my bed. "Thanks, Charlotte, thanks for believing I was ready. Thanks for letting me try."

"You're welcome. We'll practice again tomorrow, okay?"

"Great. Before you leave, I have a question—how did you get into the rehabilitation field, helping blind people?"

"Oh, didn't I tell you yesterday? I have a personal interest in blindness. I can see a little, but I'm legally blind myself.

I chuckled. I had truly experienced the blind leading the blind.

4

In Charlotte's Words: The Battle Is before Us

> *He shall say:*
> *"Hear, O Israel, today you are going into battle against your enemies. Do not be fainthearted or afraid; do not be terrified or give way to panic before them. For the LORD your God is the one who goes with you to fight for you against your enemies to give you victory."*
> *Deuteronomy 20:3-4*

I arrived at work at seven forty-five that warm May morning, and headed to my office. I'm visually impaired myself—legally blind, with about 10 percent sight. As I approached my office, I realized that two men were standing by my office door. When they greeted me, I recognized the voices of Dr. Hirst and a staff ophthalmologist.

"Well, a welcoming committee." When I got close enough to see their faces, I knew they were not there to bring me coffee and donuts.

We went into my office, and I could tell that these two men were devastated.

"Charlotte, we have a twenty-year-old male gunshot victim. His optic nerves were severed, and yesterday we enucleated both eyes. There was nothing else we could do medically. We are turning his rehabilitation over to you."

I normally worked with much older adults—patients with diabetes and degenerative vision problems—helping them cope with gradually decreasing vision. When a patient lost sight in an accident, it was usually only one eye. I understood the doctors' devastation; a healthy young man losing both eyes was tragic, and they felt helpless to do anything about it.

I wasted no time in going to visit Christopher Harvey. When I met him, I knew he was different from most of my clients. He was ready to get started with, as he put it, "learning to be blind." He didn't want to have people waiting on him, and asked me if I could help him. I was amazed when he said he wanted to be back at Shepherd College in September, and to graduate on time the next spring. With his attitude, I knew that his goal was attainable. It would take more than his effort, though, so I promised to talk with his family and develop a plan.

I can tell you that the nurses were not happy with me. They thought I was very insensitive to the fact that Chris had just lost his sight. The nurses reprimanded me when they found the ping-pong balls and cupcake tin in his room the day after his surgery, but that was nothing compared to their frustration with me when I took Chris for a walk on the second day. At that point, the nurses reported me to Dr. Hirst. When he defended me and told them that I had permission to work with Chris as I saw fit, they were furious.

I was a professional and dealt with Chris in a professional manner. I took the lead from him and presented things when he was ready. When the nurses found out I promised to help him get back into college by September, they stopped speaking to me, even refusing to acknowledge my presence for weeks after his discharge. Chris needed and wanted positive action and affirmation of his abilities, not pity over the loss of his sight.

I should have guessed that the whole Harvey family would be determined to help Chris meet his goal. Involving them in the rehab would also help them through their own grief. I assigned jobs to each one. Craig, Chris's high-school-aged brother, was in charge of summer transportation for him. He would drive Chris to doctor and rehabilitation appointments, and anywhere else he needed to go. Chris's dad, Hal, was a sales professional. I saw his strengths and put him in charge of researching speaking electronic equipment, and finding agencies to help pay for the equipment. Lucille,

Chris's mom, was to be there—as she always had been—for Chris, supporting and encouraging him as he worked toward his goal.

I only had ten days to work directly with Chris at Wilmer Eye Clinic. My job was to begin rehab, then release him to outside therapists and agencies. I would only be available after discharge to consult with the family, and to meet with Chris when he came for follow-up medical checks.

I started seeking outside assistance immediately. Unfortunately, the Maryland Department of Rehabilitation felt that newly blinded persons needed one to two years to deal with the emotional impact of losing their sight. The state would not approve monies for training until their official "mourning period and depression" were over.

If Chris wanted to return to college in barely three months, he needed to start an accelerated course of rehabilitation immediately. I knew he could handle the training; I didn't know how we would get past the bureaucracy.

Our battle was before us.

5

Rally the Troops

> *Marshal your troops,*
> *O city of troops,*
> *for a siege is laid against us.*
> *Micah 5:1a*

Charlotte was right. Getting the training that I needed to return to college in less than three months would be difficult. Although I qualified for services through the Maryland Department of Vocational Rehabilitation, there were procedural hoops and timelines to comply with, which delayed any hope of services for at least a year.

Upon hearing about this red tape, my parents' neighbors organized to raise the money to hire private Braille and mobility instructors, so I could return to Shepherd in the fall. They set a goal of four thousand dollars, which was a huge amount of money in 1980. They planned a raffle, with eight hundred tickets priced at five dollars each. The group divided into three teams. One team approached local merchants to donate items for the raffle. They quickly collected bicycles, sporting goods, televisions, and radio-alarm clocks. The second team printed and managed the ticket distribution to volunteers who would sell them. The third team managed the cash receipts and ticket stubs, and arranged a public event for the drawing.

One neighbor worked at the local ABC affiliate television station, WJLA in Washington, D.C. He secured Fred Weiss, the white-haired "grandfather of weather reporting" to be the master of ceremonies for the event. The public loved Mr. Weiss, and crowds gathered wherever he appeared.

Another community member arranged to hold the event at the Laurel Lakes Mall, The mall management allowed a booth for ticket sales during the week prior to the raffle, and offered a stage with amphitheatre seating for the event.

On the day of the raffle, the seats were full, and more onlookers surrounded the railings behind the benches. The powerful mall lighting caused the abundance of prizes to sparkle across the stage. Volunteers brought the prizes forward one at a time, and Mr. Weiss read aloud the winning numbers as they were drawn. Naturally, I was the one reaching into the basket of stubs—we joked that no one could accuse me of cheating. After awarding the prizes, Mr. Weiss introduced me to the crowd.

Although I was filled with anxiety leading up to the event, an incredible calm overtook me as I reached the podium. I thanked Mr. Weiss and all of those who worked so hard on my behalf, and shared that I was humbled by their concern for me and my family. Then, for the first time publicly, I described what had happened to me only a few weeks earlier. I explained that the proceeds of the raffle would allow me to accelerate my recovery and return to college in the fall. Even though I was not sure what future awaited me, I encouraged the crowd with my vision of graduating from Shepherd, going on to graduate school, and becoming a productive member of the business community.

The proceeds of the raffle were enough to pay for my Braille tutoring and for the training to use a cane to get around on my own. There was enough left over to purchase a Braillewriter and other needed supplies.

Remarkably, this group of neighbors brought it all together. I'd been connected with a private tutor, who graciously started my lessons before the fundraiser took place, so I did very little to assist in getting the event off the ground. These neighbors did all of the work. They were the true heroes who came to my rescue.

6

In Craig's Words: Brothers in Arms

*Be devoted to one another in brotherly love.
Honor one another above yourselves.
Romans 12:10*

My brother, Craig, gave up his summer to be my chauffeur, driving me to the Braille tutor's home in Wheaton, five days a week for six weeks. We'd arrive around noon, and my Braille lesson would last until five o'clock. I could tell you about the experience, but I think you might appreciate hearing Craig's perspective about the summer—and about my assault. When one member of a family experiences a tragedy, every member is affected. Here is Craig's recollection, starting with his return from the high school field trip, when he learned that I'd been shot.

***

Sometimes things go from bad to worse. Mom and Dad picked my girlfriend and me up at the high school when we returned from our class field trip to NYC. We took my girlfriend home, and when I carried her suitcase to the door, we found out that her grandfather had passed away a few hours earlier. I stayed about forty-five minutes, doing my best to comfort her, while Mom and Dad sat patiently in the car. When I returned, Mom got out and motioned for me to join them in the front seat. This unusual gesture made me wonder what was up, and when the car headed to the highway instead of home, I knew that something was wrong.

"We've got some bad news, buddy. Someone shot your brother, and he's in the hospital in Baltimore." Mom's words left me feeling like I'd been punched in the stomach.

"Shot? Where? What happened?" When Dad explained that the bullet hit Chris in the face, I was stunned. I imagined a bullet going through Chris's cheek and busting his jawbone. The doctors would wire the bones back and Chris would heal as good as new. During the drive, the story unraveled a little more as my parents told me about the state police coming to the house.

As we walked across the parking lot at Johns Hopkins Hospital, my anxiety level rose. The antiseptic smell of the institution hit me as we pushed through those heavy front doors. Dad turned to me. "Craig, your brother can't see.

The bullet blinded him, and he had surgery this morning to remove his eyes."

***

When I saw Chris propped up in the bed with gauze covering his head and eyes, I knew this was real. The sight was one of those defining moments when the earth seems to stand still in time, stamping a visual image that would remain in my memory forever.

What do you say in a situation like this? We chatted. Small talk. Like nothing had happened at all. When Mom and Dad were ready to go home, I asked to spend the night with Chris, so the nurses rounded up a cot for me. We had the TV on, and talked into the night, just like old times. When Johnny Carson came on, Chris said he was tired and wanted to sleep. "No need to turn the TV off, though, it won't bother me if you want to watch it."

I lowered the volume anyway and instinctively flipped the light switch off. Then it hit me: Chris was blind. The light didn't matter.

***

I guess our family dealt with things by plowing ahead, and at this point, all I wanted to do was to help Chris get back to being self-sufficient. We took our cues from Chris, and he made it clear that he wanted to get on with life. While he was still in the hospital, he told me that one of the biggest problems was not being able to tell the time of day. He'd wake in the night and think it was morning, or feel tired during the day and wonder if it was night. Sure, he could usually determine approximate times from sounds around him or when meals arrived, but it really bothered him not to know the exact time.

Dad asked Charlotte about getting a Braille watch. Charlotte's answer introduced us to the procedural guidelines of the Department of Rehabilitation. Yes, Chris qualified to receive a Braille watch, but he would first have to go away and attend special classes on how to use it. I knew he'd master the watch as quickly as he was picking up the Braille alphabet. Why would he have to go away and learn to tell time? They also wanted him to go away to learn how to eat. For crying out loud, my brother had been feeding himself for years. Even I could feed myself in the dark. I guess my frustrations with the rehabilitation system revolved around this perceived need to treat every blind person like a toddler who was learning brand new skills. Chris was smart and self-sufficient, he had the skills, and all he needed to learn were different ways of applying them. If we could get the tools and the training for him, he'd be on his way back to college by the fall.

Charlotte understood our frustrations and did everything possible to help us find private resources. She gave

Dad information about purchasing a Braille watch, and put him to work researching talking computers, which were unheard of in 1980. By the time Chris was released from Johns Hopkins in mid-May, Charlotte had our whole family mobilized with assignments for helping him meet his goal. It was evident that we were not going to get any assistance from the state rehabilitation offices for more than a year, so we went into action. My job was to be Chris's transportation, but I did more than that. Within a week of his coming home, I had him cooking. I figured that cooking was a critical life skill. Mom had taught both of us to take care of ourselves early on, and unless Chris wanted to eat cold cereal every morning, he'd better learn to fry his own eggs.

"Whack the egg on the side of the bowl as hard as you would when you could see." It didn't take much encouragement from me to get him to experiment with cracking eggs in the dark. We laughed and cleaned up more than one raw egg that didn't make it into the bowl, or flipped out of the pan when he turned it. In no time, he had a feel for the right amount of force it took to crack the shell, and the right degree of flip to make a near-perfect over-easy egg.

Charlotte had recommended a private Braille tutor who lived about a half-hour drive from our home in Laurel. The Braille lessons were four hours a day. Since the tutor preferred to work with Chris alone, I had four hours of wait time. I never traveled anywhere without my drumsticks and practice pad, so I'd drop Chris off, drive to a shady spot, and practice my drum patterns. When the sun overtook my spot, I'd go find a snack and a soda, and then drive to another shady spot. Just before five o'clock, I'd head back to the tutor's house. In the afternoon and evening, Chris would show me what he learned and I'd drill him on it. By the end of the summer, Chris had mastered a two-year curriculum of Braille instruction and I was on my way to being a professional drummer.

Even with the concentration on learning Braille and new mobility skills, we found our fun along the way. One day, we ran out of gas in my little Datsun B-210 hatchback. We were close to a gas station, so Chris opened the hatch, leaned in, and pushed the car as I pushed on my doorframe and steered. Suddenly the car crested a rise and picked up speed on the downhill. I yelled for Chris to jump in, and he dove right into the open hatchback. We laughed all the way to the station.

Chris made the best of every situation and I think that was the reason he chose to be a survivor and not a victim of his blindness. Personally, I had a hard time dealing with the details of the shooting that we'd learned over the summer: Chris's attacker was a drunken young man, randomly shooting a high-powered rifle at parked cars and houses from the hillside across from Chris's house. I even went through a period of wondering why it could not have been me instead of Chris.

The whole situation was unfair, but if Chris was ready to forgive and get on with his life, I knew that I had to let go *of my bitterness and do everything possible to support my brother. Chris's attitude inspired and empowered everyone around him. My brother saw his blindness as a stepping-stone to support others. He accepted his loss of sight as something God would work out in his life, and he knew that with God's help, everything was going to be okay.*

7

Choosing Forgiveness

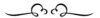

*For if you forgive men when they sin against you,
your heavenly Father will also forgive you.*
Matthew 6:14

If anyone was entitled to be angry and unforgiving, certainly I was. The first three months after my assault, I lived in survival mode and did not have the time to consider who had done this to me. But when I returned to Shepherd and moved back into the same house, the fact that I could no longer play lacrosse or football hit me again. The All-American had been red-shirted. The foul was against me, yet I was the one banished to ride the bench. I was red-shirted, not only for sports, but also for other activities that I'd always taken for granted.

The fellow who shot me was still living across the street from me—not benched like me. He'd been released on bail almost as quickly as he'd been arrested. He was drinking that night in May, and standing on the hillside across from my front porch, he'd shot a hunting rifle at houses and streetlights. He was a disturbed young man—close to my age—who lived with his parents in the house across the road. It wasn't fair that he was free while awaiting trial, but I was not afraid of him. I felt confident that he posed no further danger to me.

But then Satan wedged a boulder of outrage onto the path of hope that I'd chosen to follow. *I'm not worried about this guy, but is it time for him to worry about me?* The entitlement to anger stung me like a thwacked rubber band: *I'm being a wimp.* Something stirred inside of me, calling for trouble, seeking justice, and demanding retribution.

I raged about the injustice and emotionally exploded. What happened to me was incredibly unfair. It was my responsibility to take my anger out on someone, somehow. Maybe blowing the steam off would ease the anguish I felt.

With two of my friends looking on, I stepped onto the front porch of the house and stood at the wrought iron railing. I flailed my fists in the air and screamed at the young man up the hill. Even though I saw nothing, I easily pictured the hillside and his house in my mind. I felt no fear and had every right to be angry.

Then something burst. My actions were totally out of character for me, and I wondered what I was doing. My desperate need to be the roaring lion vanished. The mood snapped and peace settled in. I was not looking for peace, but I had no control over it, because at that instant, God imposed it. He imposed it with a love that embraced me and gently turned me toward forgiveness.

I felt stupid. Maybe that was how Adam and Eve felt when God showed them their nakedness. I was ashamed of my foolish display. I had so much more to spew, but the wave of holiness extinguished the resentful demon within me. Hatred toward my assailant would have bound me in spiritual blindness. Forgiveness opened my eyes to see and receive the blessings that God still held for my future.

8

Moving Forward

No weapon formed against you shall prosper.
Isaiah 54:17

On another day, I was at the house alone. I walked into the living room and slid my hands along the paneled wall. *Where's the bullet hole? I can't believe that the property owner only patched it and didn't replace the paneling. Of course, with the rent we're paying, he probably couldn't afford it.* Then my fingers hit it—the rough patch of wood putty that plugged the hole. *This is it?* I'd imagined much more damage, based on the splinters and insulation that burst into the room with the bullet. *Kind of like my wounds—not much on the outside, but robbing me of sight for the rest of my life.*

The furniture had been rearranged, so I pulled a chair to the spot where I'd been shot. As I sat down, my mind replayed the sound of the initial gunshots. My heart raced, pumping adrenaline through my body, just as it had during the moments before I was hit. Did the porch light and glow from the window attract my assailant, as he stood on that hillside? Did he slowly scan the houses and deliberately pick his targets? In slow motion, I imagined the path that the bullet must have taken. I traced its trail—from the chamber, out the barrel of the rifle, over the field, across the street, through the wall, through my head, and out the back wall of the living room.

I sat there, bathed in melancholy memories, not angry or sad, but somewhat bewildered. What were the odds that a bullet would take this precise path? How did the bullet breach the clapboard and the inner paneling, and then precisely travel behind my eyes, severing my optic nerves? A half-inch back would have killed me or caused brain damage. The bullet entered so cleanly that my external wounds only required a few stitches. My sight was taken with no less precision than if surgeons had done the deed in an operating room.

I knew that God's angels were guiding that bullet. I believe angels had been in position since the day I moved in, watching and waiting to keep me from being killed, maimed, or disfigured in this attack. I knew that God would continue to protect me and would provide the strength I needed to live the rest of my life without sight.

I am not sure what drove my curiosity to retrace those moments, but I can tell you that doing so helped me to bring closure to the shooting. After reliving the memory, I felt as if I had visited a graveyard and touched the tombstone of someone who had not yet died. God had brought me through the ordeal alive, and I wanted to live my life, not walk among the dead.

***

I was ready to move on, but even though I made peace with the event and the place where I lost my sight, I still had to deal with the fact that I was blind. My twenty-first birthday arrived on September 27, 1980, about a month after my return to Shepherd College and to the house in Sharpsburg. I celebrated this "coming of age" milestone outwardly, but it was a reminder that I would spend my entire adult life unable to see. The longevity of my loss affected me more than I had expected. Again, I had a choice to make. I could allow my life sentence to shatter my psyche, or I could refuse to dwell on things I could not change. I can best describe my feelings on that birthday as standing on a cliff and looking over the edge into an abyss of churning evil—anger, bitterness, hatred, and most of all, self-pity. The Spirit of God protected me from that abyss. The love of Jesus strengthened me to choose hope, make the best of my situation, and continue moving forward—a choice that I would have to reaffirm every day of my life. God made the impression on me that I would be storing treasures in heaven by using my loss of sight to inspire others. Understanding that I would have restored sight in heaven helped me to find peace to handle the enormity of my situation.

9

The Victory Belongs to the Lord

What, then, shall we say in response to this?
If God is for us, who can be against us?
Romans 8:31

I had become an interesting combination of celebrity and novelty. In May, I was the ordinary college student; in September, I was someone everyone talked about and wanted to know. My classmates were amazed that I survived the bullet, and they could not believe that I was back already. Students and faculty embraced me and offered support. This new high profile was a kind of fame I never sought, but it was my destiny.

I was also a novelty, since few of the people on campus personally knew a blind person. The funny part is that they were learning how to act around me and I was simply learning how to act. I was changing gears—adapting to life without sight—and my classmates were along for the ride, learning how to relate to me. I am thankful that I had a good attitude, despite my circumstances. References to sight are a natural part of our language, and often people would ask me if I'd seen a movie or if I'd seen a certain person lately. Then they'd be embarrassed and apologize for the comments. I didn't want others to be anxious about making visual references when we were having a conversation, so I took a light-hearted approach. I remembered the easy manner in which Mr. Miller, the man who made my artificial eyes, had joked with me about blindness. "Hey, Chris," he'd said, "how about I make you an extra pair of artificial eyes that are blood-shot, for the morning after?" His sense of humor made me more comfortable, and perhaps my jovial attitude would help others be more comfortable with my blindness. So, did I see that new movie? No, but I heard it was great.

***

My Lambda Chi Alpha fraternity brothers welcomed me back, and offered to relieve me of my duties as vice-president of the fraternity if I thought it would be too much. But I stayed on to prove to everyone, and to myself, that I was still reliable and could get things done. My closest fraternity brothers helped me with rides, guidance in finding the classes on my new schedule, and trips to the Ram's Den in the student union for a bite to eat.

One brother in particular, Steve Ames, made sure that I was still included in activities. Once he took his girlfriend to a theme park and insisted that I come along. It was the first time I'd been to an amusement park since losing my sight, and I asked Steve to lead me to a bench when he announced that the roller coaster was next on our agenda.

"Come on, you can do it. We don't want to leave you here on the bench while we're having fun."

"Are you crazy? I've been terrified of heights and of roller coasters all of my life. There is no way I'm getting on that monster with you."

"Aw, come on, Chris. You can shut your eyes."

That did it. I started to laugh, and the next thing I knew, Steve was ushering me into a cold metal roller coaster car. I slid across the stiff vinyl seat and grasped the bar that closed down into my lap. Steve and his girl climbed into the car in front of me.

"You're gonna love this, Chris. Now relax and feel the wind on your face."

"Yeah. Sure." The coaster lurched forward, the rails creaked as we crept up the first hill, and the force of gravity pulled me deeper into the seat. Then we crested that first rise, and dropped. As soon as my stomach slid back down from my throat, I shouted, "Wahoo." What a blast. The park wasn't crowded that day, so we must have ridden that roller coaster a dozen times in a row. I had a lot of catching up to do.

***

Of course, fraternity activities and trips to amusement parks weren't my focus when I returned to school. My goal of graduating on time was the most important thing to me. Most professors accommodated my needs. I was expected to learn the same information, but the written tests were read aloud or recorded for me to listen to. I had to make a concerted effort to organize my thoughts and arrange materials in my head before answering orally, recording, or typing my answers.

Instead of only my books, a pen, and notebook, I now had to tote a backpack full of equipment to class—cassette recorders and tapes; electrical cords; a talking calculator; a metal Braille slate, stylus, and Braille paper. For my class assignments or research projects, I'd use three or four tape recorders and compile different types of information on each recorder. I'd listen to these orally organized notes—often spending hours forwarding and rewinding the tapes to find the information I needed—and compose the final draft on another tape recorder. Then I'd hire a typist to transcribe the paper for me, since I was not able to see and correct typos on my Smith-Corona typewriter.

Taking Braille notes by hand was cumbersome because it required punching a stylus through paper into cells on a metal slate to create the raised dots. Since I was embossing the paper from the back, I Brailled right to left as well as forming the letters in reverse—like mirror writing. I then flipped the paper so that the raised punches could be read from left to right. Fortunately, I soon discovered that I was an auditory learner, and if I listened intently in class, I retained more than when I took notes in Braille. Without visual distractions, I could concentrate completely on the lecture and commit most of the information to memory.

***

My senior year seemed to speed by, and it neared time for final exams. I was proud that I'd meet my goal of graduating on schedule, but as I sat on the porch of our house studying, I questioned my future. I recalled hanging out on the porch a year earlier—it had been my favorite spot to drag a kitchen chair and sit. My roomies would usually be inside watching TV, but I loved being outside in God's world. I'd sit there reading the *Wall Street Journal*—the newspaper that represented my dream of pursuing a business career—poring over the pages, reading every article with the same fervor that I'd studied my business textbooks. I had a clear recollection of those intimate times, when the wind blew the smell of flowers toward me as I pondered future possibilities, with the statistics of the world's wealth in my lap. Now, without my sight, I wondered if it would be possible to succeed in a career that depended on staying current on the news. Would I be able to keep up with all of the changing information if I was no longer able to read this daily publication?

As I questioned my future, a gentle breeze brought a new bouquet of fragrances from the field across the street. The scent of lilac and honeysuckle filled my senses and repainted vivid mental pictures of the field that I had gazed upon one year ago. Back then, I'd thought of it as another common, over-grown field. Now I remembered what a beautiful hillside it was, and I wished I'd spent more time appreciating the beauty when I could see. Black-eyed Susans graced the edge of the field that bordered our narrow street. Behind them was a crippled and rusty barbed-wire fence, wrapped in honeysuckle and raspberry thickets. The hill dipped beyond the old fence line and then ascended again, bordered at the top by another forgotten fence and a line of trees that touched the horizon. No doubt, the field had been cultivated at some time, but nature had reclaimed it years ago. I imagined it tall with green stalks of corn in the past, and now carpeted with grass, raspberries, and honeysuckle. Was the cultivated field better than the wild one? No, they were different, but each had a beauty and a value of its own. That's how I had to look at my life: it was different now, but it could be just as productive.

***

The Shepherd College Commencement Ceremony for the Class of 1981 was scheduled a few days after the last exams. My family members, Charlotte Seltser, and her husband, Ray, were in the audience to watch me receive my diploma. The ceremony took place in the football stadium, and Senator Byrd spoke to the class. I'd asked my brother Craig to sit with me and escort me across the stage. Finally, the time came for the "H's" to move into position to receive their diplomas. Craig tapped my arm when the silent cue came for our row to rise.

I bristled with excitement and pride when the president called out my name, "Christopher Howell Harvey." As Craig walked me across the stage, the audience broke into a whooping standing ovation. This thirty-second party was a short celebration of a community sharing in my victory. They were witnesses to, as well as being a part of, an unbelievable triumph. I turned and waved, but I knew that my success was only possible by the grace of God. I felt his presence and sensed his pleasure in providing this victory. I pictured him looking down from heaven and smiling as I walked across that stage. It was not Christopher Howell Harvey who was in charge, but the loving heavenly Father who directed my path. The victory belonged to the Lord.

10

Walking By Dog

─⌒⌒─

> *God said, "Let us make man in our image,*
> *in our likeness, and let them rule over*
> *the fish of the sea and the birds of the air,*
> *over the livestock, over all the earth,*
> *and over all the creatures*
> *that move along the ground."*
> *Genesis 1:26*

A few weeks after graduation, I took my next step towards independence: I attended training to work with a dog guide. Instructor Peter Lange met me at the airport in Newark, New Jersey, the closest airport to the Seeing Eye facility in Morristown.

"Stay right here, Chris. You're the first of the students in my group to arrive. I have to round up the others coming in on different flights. Don't move from here—I'll be right back."

So began my boot camp of sorts at the Seeing Eye for the Blind. My palms sweated as I awaited Peter's return. One by one, Peter guided the others to my spot. When we had all gathered, Peter retrieved his van and we all piled in. Two men on my team were from the states, and there was a man from Spain, and a woman from Canada. We were strangers, but over the next month, we would become a team, working with Peter and with the dogs that would be matched to our individual needs and personalities. Even under the circumstances that brought me there, I was grateful for the opportunity to learn to work with a dog. With my plans to start graduate school in the fall, and my intention of having my own townhouse without roommates, a dog guide would allow me the independence that I desired. God's four-legged friend of mankind would serve as my surrogate eyes—the thought thrilled me.

***

It was a short ride to Morristown, and I found myself in a dormitory similar to what I'd experienced my first year at Shepherd College. There were four other trainers, besides Mr. Lange, and about thirty students enrolled for the month-long training. We stayed on the second floor with a common area separating the men and the women. Each room housed two, with twin beds on opposite walls. Tie-down chains for the dogs were anchored into the baseboard at the head of each bed, but we would not receive our dogs until we'd completed several days of classroom training.

As soon as we'd all unpacked, we met for a tour of the grounds and an introduction to the history of the dog guide program. We learned that the Seeing Eye in Morristown, founded in the early 1920s by a female German immigrant, was the first dog guide school in the United States. The facility covered many manicured acres and housed its own kennels and veterinary clinic. This prestigious establishment still held to the prim and proper formalities of the early twentieth century. Perhaps the founder thought that blind people needed training in etiquette, or perhaps she wanted the trainees to experience pampering and luxury to offset the hard work that was before them. Whatever the reason, mealtime was a formal affair. We dined on fine china with sterling silverware and crystal goblets. Gentlemen were required to wear dinner jackets—and in case they forgot to bring one along, a rack of "loaners" was located outside the dining hall. I headed to dinner one time without my jacket. Forgetting it that once was one time too many—the clerk at the checkroom had to dig through the loaners to find a jacket close to my size.

I teased, "Hey, what difference does a dinner jacket make anyway? Who is going to see me?" The lack of laughter told me that he'd probably heard that lame blind joke many times. I squeezed my broad shoulders into the snug jacket and headed to the dining room door. No jacket, no entry into the dining room—that was the rule. I never forgot my own jacket again—it wasn't worth it to jeopardize my next meal there.

***

During the first day of training, Mr. Lange dispelled the common myths about dog guides so that we could better understand our role as director of the human/dog team. Often people think that the dog makes the decision to cross the road, based on traffic lights. First, dogs are colorblind and see in only shades of black, white, and grey, so they are not able to distinguish the colors on a traffic signal. Second, they are trained to focus on the regions immediately to the left and right of their master, the area for head clearance, and obstacles in the footpath. The dogs tend to ignore items beyond this sort of "strike zone," so even if they were able to figure out that the top light was "stop" and the bottom light was "go," they wouldn't be looking for it. Instead, the master listens for the traffic pattern to tell when the lights change. For instance, if the team is traveling north on the east side of the street and comes to a curb, they stop for the master to listen. If traffic is moving left to right in front of them, they wait for that east-west traffic to stop. When these cars come to a stop and the cars on the team's left start to move out, the light is presumed to have turned green and the master gives the verbal "forward" command, accompanied with the forward hand signal. The dogs were trained to refuse to go, and would even wrap their heads around our knees to stop us if they detected danger, like a car turning a corner, or an obstacle to our path, such as street construction. A popular misconception is that the dogs are deciding where to go, but that is the master's job and requires that the master have knowledge of how to reach his destination. A tactile map helped us learn the layout of the Seeing Eye facility and the local neighborhoods and shopping areas where our training would take us. Similar to a relief globe, these flat maps were made of layers of wood and plastic and had three-dimensional landmarks. One route that I quickly learned was to the local coffee and donut shop.

***

Holding a dog harness as if he were the dog, Mr. Lange introduced each of us to "Juno," the invisible dog guide. When it was my turn, I grasped the handle of the harness with my left hand and followed the gentle pull of his lead. When we arrived at a step, "Juno" slowed to a stop. "There are two steps down, Chris. I'm telling you this time, but next time you'll need to slide your foot forward and determine what the obstacle might be." So, with the warning from Mr. Lange, I gave "Juno" the forward command. "Juno" didn't move. I'd forgotten to give the hand signal as well.

"Forward," I commanded again. This time I motioned forward by moving my hand in the direction I wanted my dog to go. "Juno" led me on. This training with Mr. Lange pretending to be the guide dog allowed me to get the sense of working with a dog. I soon learned the feel of the harness as "Juno" walked to the left or the right, and adjusted my path to follow. Likewise, a downward tug of the harness let me know that the dog was stepping down and repeated tugs meant a series of steps. For the first four days at Seeing Eye, we practiced each morning and afternoon with "Juno," the invisible dog guide, going through the different verbal and hand commands, climbing stairs, stepping off curbs, and finding our way back to the dining hall or dormitory.

Mr. Lange had trained the five dogs for the members of my group. The four days he spent working with us allowed him to make the final dog assignments to match each of our personalities.

***

At last the big day came. Instead of going to the training room after breakfast, we returned to our dormitory rooms. My heart raced as wildly as it had when I was a child anticipating what Santa left under the tree. Only this time, instead of jumping out of my bed and running to find out, I had to sit patiently and wait for the surprise to come to me.

The trainers each brought one dog at a time to meet its new master. With the dogs huffing down the hall, and barking in excitement about going into a new place, the trainers running around, and the students shouting, laughing, and sometimes crying, the dormitory took on a circus-like atmosphere. My roommate received one of the first dogs delivered—a cute black Lab named Brandy. I sat on the edge of my bed, listening to him play with her, but I focused my attention on the door to the room. It wasn't as if I'd see it swing open, but the first sound of the doorknob would be my audio key. Finally, the huffing and puffing mutt I'd heard coming down the hall stopped at my door. Mr. Lange flung the door open, led the prancing dog to my bed, and pressed the leash into my hand.

"Chris, meet Baron." At that moment, Baron jumped onto my bed, knocked me over backwards, and then proceeded to lick my face. He then twisted away and romped about the room.

I pulled myself up and laughed. "Mr. Lange, is that wild creature supposed to guide me? You had better wish me luck."

Mr. Lange retrieved the rambunctious Baron and returned the leash to my hands. "He's a beautiful shepherd with a black back, fading into silver on his sides, and tan on his tummy and paws. And his face has a beautiful shepherd's mask."

"Shepherd's mask? What's that?"

"He's black around the eyes and back to his ears—almost like Zorro's mask. The rest of his face is tan. "

"Wow. He sounds great. "

"Yes, he's a handsome dog. He's also a great deal larger and older than the other dogs. He's a retired international show dog."

Now that was cool—my dog was a champion. It didn't matter to me that he was three-and-a-half years old and weighed twenty pounds more than the typical dog guide. I guess the biggest guy in the group would naturally get the biggest dog.

Thirty blind folks with the same number of rookie dog guides made for some interesting first days. The average dog was only about sixteen to eighteen months old and full of puppy energy. Not only were the dogs distracted by each other and the commotion, they were still attached to and looking for their trainers.

Within a few days, though, Baron and the other dogs settled down. It was a learning process for both of us, but soon Baron was following my commands to go through the paces that Mr. Lange had taught him earlier. As a team, I would take a few steps forward with Baron on the leash. I'd then stop or suddenly step back a pace or two, slap my hip with my right hand, and call out, "Baron, come, " then, "heel. " Baron would circle around behind me, and then step into position at my left side. Usually before I'd even give the next command, "sit," he'd anticipate and begin to sit down. I would then say "down" and apply a little pressure on his leash. "Lay down." The procedure ended with Baron laying by my left foot and in perfect control. I'd then slap my left hip and command, "up," and Baron would sit up at my side. "Good boy." I'd then rub his head and neck to reward this cooperative behavior. We used doggy treats early on, but we quickly transitioned to using affection and attention as the ultimate reward.

***

To avoid collisions with each other, the students would call out, "Coming down the hall, coming down the hall, Chris and Baron are coming down the hall," to communicate our pathways to others. When the weather was nice, we could spread out over the campus to practice these walking drills, but on rainy days, the building turned into a zoo. Repeated trips up and down corridors, passing each team on the right, required that we know our distance from one another to avoid collisions, but thirty people repeating the same phrase can start to drive you nuts.

Reveille was at five thirty each morning, for "park time," when we'd feed and walk our dogs. Breakfast followed at seven o'clock in the main dining room, and at eight o'clock, our group would meet with Mr. Lange to learn the itinerary for the day. Sometimes we'd train on the campus, other times we'd pile into a van and go into town or the neighborhoods to practice our skills with the dogs. The merchants and residents of Morristown were accustomed to students at the Seeing Eye using their sidewalks and stores as training grounds. We were encouraged to go into the stores to purchase personal items, and into the food establishments for meals. The local waiters and waitresses knew to look out for puppy tails as they served us at the coffee shop and in the restaurants. These excursions into town gave us practice in having our dogs heel and sit patiently by our side as we made purchases, and in guiding us as we traveled along the sidewalks from one destination to another. The trainers would intentionally place broken limbs, trashcans, and other obstacles along the prescribed course, so that the team could learn to handle them. Advanced training included boarding buses and trains. A special trip to the mall gave us practice in handling escalators, elevators, ramps, and staircases.

***

After four long weeks of training, I was anxious and excited when it was time to go home. I beamed with pride as the plane circled Baltimore Washington International airport in the landing approach. I'd endured a month of training and was coming home with skills that most people would never experience. And I was coming home with Baron, my new companion and guide.

11

On My Own, But Not Alone

*Be strong and courageous.
Do not be afraid or terrified because of them,
for the LORD your God goes with you;
he will never leave you nor forsake you.
Deuteronomy 31:6*

The next step was to earn my Master's degree before embarking upon my career. I decided that my ability to tutor fellow students at Shepherd in economics gave me good odds of success studying this field for my graduate degree. I applied to Penn State, Duke, and the University of Virginia.

While I awaited responses from these schools, my dad stopped at the University of Virginia, while on a business trip in the area, and met with the assistant dean of economics.

The dean listened intently as Dad related my story, but then he said, "I'm sorry to hear about your son's tragedy, and I am amazed that he returned to Shepherd and graduated with honors. However, I would have to discourage advanced studies in economics." He explained, "Economics includes three-dimensional graphs, calculus, and other visual challenges. I'm sorry, but I don't believe our department is a suitable choice for a blind person."

My dad came home disheartened over the dean's remarks. They had the opposite effect on me, though. I loved a challenge. The dean did not know Christopher Howell Harvey. I knew I could handle the coursework with a few accommodations.

When acceptances to all three universities arrived, I knew where I'd go. I would show that I could overcome any visual challenges to earning a degree in economics. I was going to UVA and study economics to prove that a blind man could succeed in that field.

***

When I returned home with my new dog guide, Baron, Dad and I went to Charlottesville to look for housing and to get me registered for the fall semester. We walked and we walked, often building to building with misinterpreted directions, but we gathered the necessary forms and completed the initial processes required by one of the most historic colleges in the nation. We organized books and articles from lists the professors provided for each class and quickly turned them over to the Recording for the Blind studio (RFB) to tape before my classes began. The location of an RFB studio in Charlottesville was a bonus to my decision to attend UVA. Finally, we checked out apartments and townhouses within walking distance of my classroom buildings, and settled on a townhouse on John Street.

***

On moving day, my parents drove me to Charlottesville. We all knew the gravity of what was about to happen, yet we were trying to be positive. When I returned to Shepherd, I returned to friends and a familiar campus. How would I make it in a strange place on my own? I wanted to share my fears and concerns with my parents, and no doubt, they wanted to share their feelings with me. But only random conversation buffered the several-hour trip. It seems so crazy that in those times of needing to communicate our deepest feelings and anxieties, we all tend to resort to courteous superficial banter.

We arrived at my new apartment and unpacked my belongings. Soon it was time for my parents to say good-bye and head home. It was time for me to begin a new chapter of my life on my own.

As strong as I'd imagined myself, I was not prepared for the emotional impact of moving into a house without roommates. After my parents left, I sat in the middle of my living room, on a wheeled desk chair, with Baron faithfully at my side. I sat and cried. What had I done? It was just me—a blind guy and a dog. And I knew absolutely no one in Charlottesville. I had positioned myself for this next challenge, but what kind of challenge had I created?

The fear and overwhelming sadness made me want to go back home with my parents. In fact, Mom called from Dad's car phone when they had only gone a few miles out of town. "How about we come back and pick you up? Or maybe I will stay with you for a few days, and your father can come back and pick me up next week?"

This offer was a crossroad. I longed to have them come back and take me home, but how grounded was I in my resolve to be independent? God had been with me through everything else, he would strengthen me now. He gave me the courage to say, "I know this is hard, Mom. It's very, very hard. But we have to do this eventually. We're this far underway, let's try to give it a few days. I'll call you and Dad tonight, okay?"

I was on my own—but not alone. God did not bring me this far to leave me nor forsake me.

12

Blazing the Brokerage Trail

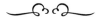

*For we are God's workmanship,
created in Christ Jesus to do good works,
which God prepared in advance for us to do.
Ephesians 2:10*

"Chris, have you ever considered a career as a stock broker? You have a remarkable understanding of business operations and you keep up with all the current events in the financial markets." Howard Kaylor's question was a turning point in my life.

Howard worked for a regional brokerage firm, Ferris & Company, in Hagerstown, Maryland. With the small financial settlement from my assailant's parents' homeowners' policy, I'd ventured into the stock market and invested with Howard.

"I'm not qualified—"

"Sure you are. You're finishing up your master's in economics—and besides, many of the most successful brokers don't even have a college degree."

Howard arranged for me to interview with the regional manager in the Bethesda office.

Prior to my job search, my father helped me research computers that could read text. I found a Hewlett Packard modified with voice synthesis by Maryland Computer Services. This first generation talking computer cost fourteen thousand dollars in 1982. It's a good thing I didn't need a car—because that was about the price of a new one at the time. Even though this was a costly investment, I knew I needed it to make myself more marketable in the financial world. After all, if I was not willing to invest in myself, who would?

I went into the interview with Ferris & Company, hopeful that my degree and the talking computer would help me land the job. The interview did not go as well as I anticipated. I was administered a preliminary aptitude test and then taken into the manager's office. I sat in the chair across from his desk, and Baron settled at my feet.

"You did very well on the test, Mr. Harvey, but I have to be frank with you. If I lost my sight tomorrow, there is no way that I could compete as a broker. I suggest that you first prove yourself by going into insurance sales."

I could not believe what I was hearing. *Great. He won't give me an opportunity to prove myself selling securities from a phone at a desk—and he thinks I should go door-to-door selling insurance in people's homes?* I tried not to bristle, but with a measured tone, I thanked him and then said, "One day, every broker in the metropolitan area will know who I am." Then Baron and I left the office. My retort and attitude resulted from my annoyance with this discrimination and from overconfidence in the young buck that I was. I was discouraged, but I'd faced discrimination before, and it fueled my determination to prove myself.

***

I continued interviewing and received an offer with Thompson McKinnon, an old-line brokerage firm. But before accepting the job, I decided to follow up on a suggestion that came from an acquaintance at Recording for the Blind. She told me that Jim Wheat, president of Wheat First Securities, was blind. She suggested I apply for a position there.

I contacted Mr. Wheat's personal secretary, Jane Brook, in the corporate offices located in Richmond, Virginia. Mrs. Brook relayed my information to Mr. Wheat, who scheduled an interview with Jack Call, the manager of Wheat's Bethesda, Maryland office.

Finally, the day for my interview arrived. Little did I know that Jack Call would become my mentor, and that his influence would shape the broker I was to become. After hearing my story, Jack was amazed at how I recovered from the assault. "Chris, you have the drive to succeed at whatever you set your sights on. And I'm quite impressed with your talking computer package."

The next step was an interview in Richmond. Mr. Call set that up and drove me down. Any manager who would take an entire day off work to get me to, and through, the Richmond interview was the kind of man I wanted to work for. The interview day started early with a stop in Fredericksburg, Virginia for me to take a battery of personality and intelligence exams. Then we headed to Richmond, where I'd go through a series of interviews, and finally, I'd meet Mr. Jim Wheat.

The interviews went pretty well, until about halfway through my time with the vice-president of operations, Mr. Macke. "Now where did you say you lived?" When I told him I lived in Laurel, Maryland, he swiveled in his chair and unrolled a wall map of Maryland. "Hmmm. Now let me see, where is Laurel? I see Baltimore, where is it in relationship to there?"

I responded, "About ten or fifteen miles south, down I-95. The crossroad is Route 216."

Mr. Macke went on to quiz me. "I see Route 32, and over here is Route 29, but no Route 216."

"Really?" I queried.

"Yeah. I see Burtonsville and Beltsville, but not Laurel."

Young, anxious, and not realizing that he was testing my ability to relate visual information to others, I simply replied, "Sir, I think you need a new map. Laurel was founded at least one hundred years ago and it is right where you are looking."

He chuckled and said, "You're probably right."

Throughout the day, I met with many other directors and department heads. Finally, Mr. Call and I were ushered into Jim Wheat's corner office, with windowed walls overlooking the James River and downtown Richmond. To me, this was as exciting as entering the Oval Office to meet the President of the United States. I was nervous, but Mr. Wheat's demeanor quickly put me at ease. He'd just finished his workout on the exercise bicycle in the corner of his office, and he casually engaged Mr. Call in conversation. It was August 1982, and he quipped that he hoped the recent Dow Jones rally was the start of something that might last this time.

We all sat down, and I explained to the blind chairman how my talking computer worked, and how it would help me as a broker. He laughed and said that he was too old of a dog to learn new tricks like that. Our twenty-minute visit was just that, not a formal interview. I'll always remember Mr. Wheat's comment as we were preparing to leave: "Chris, my boy, you'll do fine in this business. Your only problem is that you went to the wrong school." Jim Wheat had graduated from the University of Virginia's rival, Virginia Military Institute.

***

Wheat First Securities hired me as a broker trainee in the Bethesda branch in October of 1982, and I spent my first two months of employment preparing for my Series Seven license exam. My first challenge was to get the study materials from two huge three-ring binders recorded onto cassette tapes as quickly as possible. I called on the Recording for the Blind studio in Charlottesville, and the Recording Services for the Visually Handicapped in Falls Church, Virginia for help. The odd-numbered chapters were shipped to Charlottesville, and the even-numbered ones went to Falls Church. This odd/even system allowed the readers at the two locations to get the earliest chapters back to me quickly. By the time I'd studied a few chapters, they would have another batch ready for me.

While awaiting the tapes, I went back to work on my master's thesis, which had been shelved in the process of my moving from Charlottesville to my new townhouse in Laurel, and during my job interviews. I concentrated on finishing this crucial ticket to my degree for about two weeks, and then the Series Seven tapes started arriving in waves.

I was flattered that the New York Stock Exchange flew the head of their testing department to Bethesda in December to give me the exam. He was a gracious gentleman who put me at ease, and even graded my test before his flight home. As he was leaving, he congratulated both Mr. Call and me. I had scored a ninety-one and my certificate would be mailed within a day or two.

***

One week after that exam, I returned to Charlottesville to defend my thesis. Then, in January, I went to Richmond for a month-long extensive broker-training course with twenty other new brokers from around the Mid-Atlantic States.

The course ended during what became the blizzard of 1983. Anxious to get home, the fellow broker I rode with thought we should try to beat the storm. We became snowbound when the interstate closed, and spent a night sleeping in the lobby of a hotel along with many other stranded travelers.

When I finally arrived home, I crashed. I was exhausted, both physically and mentally, after several months of intense training. But I was now "street legal." I had my license, and received my first producer representative number of 397. I was in business finally, and, I was eager to blaze the brokerage trail. Near the end of my rookie year, *Registered Representative* magazine did a feature story on me for pioneering talking computers in the brokerage industry.

And remember the broker who wanted me to prove myself by selling insurance before he would consider hiring me? Well, he read the article and phoned to congratulate me. His words, "I wish I had seen beyond your disability and given you the chance to prosper in our company," caused me to change my mind about him, too. I graciously thanked him for calling, and wished him the best in his career. It took a good man to humble himself and admit when he made a mistake.

13

Soul Mate

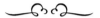

A wife of noble character who can find?
She is worth far more than rubies.
Her husband has full confidence in her
and lacks nothing of value.
She brings him good, not harm,
all the days of her life.
Proverbs 31:10-12

My fraternity brother, Joe, phoned me at work one afternoon. "Hey Chris, who is the king of trivia for radio contests? Man, I won four—yes, four—tickets to the Bayou in Georgetown for the Kim Mitchell Band. Are you free on Saturday night?"

I smiled. Good old Joe took the brotherhood pledge seriously. He lived close to me, and often included me as a threesome when he and his girlfriend went out. "Hey, that sounds great, but you have four tickets—"

"Not to worry, man. I already have a date for you. A blind date."

"And does the lovely young girl know how blind her blind date is?"

"Yes, she works with Elizabeth, and she's tired of hearing second-hand about the amazing blind guy who tags along with us on the weekends. Oh, her name is Stephanie."

Saturday night came, and Joe described Stephanie's outfit to me as the girls approached the car. I nearly bailed. A tiger-striped blouse and matching shoes? What was I thinking? Was she going to be too wild or too "out there" for me?

Then Joe added, "Oh, and she is beautiful." So much for worrying about tiger stripes—or bailing.

***

Even though I had dated since losing my sight, I had not had a crush on a girl in years. After that first date with Stephanie, I wondered if she was the one. We began chatting on the phone daily, and had a few get-to-know-you dates. On one of the first dinners out, I took on my business-like nature and got down to the basics right away. We were having burgers and fries at the local Hamburger Hamlet, and I asked her a frank question about her career plans and her life ambitions.

There was a moment of silence—as if she thought I was off my rocker. She sighed, and then said, "My goal is to get the catsup out of this bottle."

There she was, sitting next to me, my soul mate. A woman I already thought I might love, who did not try to snow me with ambitions of being a corporate CEO. There was something overwhelming about our developing relationship. We were like two magnets drawn together by an unseen force. I didn't understand the depth of God working in my life at that point, but he was bringing us together as one flesh and one soul from the second we met. Cupid's arrow had pierced my heart, and I knew Stephanie was the one. I could not spend a moment without her on my mind. And approaching six months of dating, I proposed to her.

***

In my years at Shepherd College, the Bavarian Inn, which overlooks the Potomac River, had captured my romantic imagination and that was where I wanted to pop the question. I called ahead to let the staff know my intentions, and requested their best table and service. As it turned out, we got the table that was easiest for the staff to observe us.

We selected our meal from the menu, and before the first course arrived, I was bursting with excitement. I could not put off the moment any longer. I forgot to get down on one knee, as I had mentally practiced for years in anticipation of the quintessential moment. I reached toward the right, where Stephanie was sitting and she immediately grasped my hand. Ignoring the feeling that my face was contorted from fear, I asked the question I'd rehearsed enough not to forget.

"Stephanie, will you marry me and have my children?"

She responded, "Are you serious?"

I could not speak and doubt flowed through every cell of my being. Was she going to turn me down? The thought had never crossed my mind until that moment.

Then she said, "Yes, I'll marry you and have your children."

I reached into my pocket and pulled out the box with the shiny symbol of my love. Opening it, I turned toward her and said, "Then this is for you."

With both of our hands shaking, I slid the ring onto her finger and blurted, "I love you, baby."

And she replied, "I love you, too."

The dining room erupted into applause as the staff cheered and poured champagne for everyone in the room.

One year later, on November 1, 1986, we were married in a candlelight ceremony in the church my family had attended since Craig and I were kids. Our reception was at the La Fountain Bleu in Lanham, Maryland. It was a wonderful sit down dinner with a live band, cutting of the wedding cake, and tossing of the garter. Our first dance as husband and wife was to Joe Crocker's "You Are So Beautiful." We spent most of the evening posing for pictures and talking to our guests, but when the band kicked into "Old Time Rock and Roll," we snuck away to the dance floor. The crowd was hopping. You could feel the celebration in the air that night.

***

We honeymooned in Jamaica and stayed at the Eden II resort in Ocho Rios. My new wife was brave enough to climb Dunn River Falls with me and sail down the Martha Brae River on a tour-guided bamboo raft trip. Wherever we went in Jamaica, the natives were amazed that Stephanie married me. In their country, the disabled are shunned and never expected to be productive members of society. Not only was it revolutionary that Stephanie married a blind man, the Jamaicans could not fathom that I was a stockbroker. They called that "a fancy job" and continued to marvel that a beautiful woman like Stephanie would choose to marry a blind man. Actually, she did not choose to marry a blind man; she chose to marry a man who happened to be blind.

14

In Stephanie's Words: Blind Date

*He has taken me to the banquet hall, and his banner
over me is love.
Song of Solomon 2:4*

I was between boyfriends, working three evenings a week at Ruby Tuesday's and full-time in the personnel office at the Marriott. My coworker, Elizabeth, entertained me every Monday with stories of dinners and movies with Joe and his blind friend, Chris. I'd hear "Chris did this" and "Chris did that." Honestly, my curiosity was killing me, so when Elizabeth came over to my desk that day and told me about the four tickets and needing a date for him, I said yes. It might be fun to go to the Bayou with a blind guy and see if he really was as amazing as Elizabeth said.

I changed clothes several times that night before deciding on the tiger stripes and denim—it was the eighties, and I liked being fashionable. Even though he couldn't see what I was wearing, I wanted to look nice for him.

We had a good time on the date, and Chris asked me to go to dinner with him the following week. Since we worked close together, he asked if I would pick him up at his office before the date.

***

On the appointed afternoon, I left work and drove to his office. When I walked into the building, Chris greeted me with, "You look beautiful in blue. I especially like the contrasting black buttons and belt. Wow."

I stopped in my tracks and said, "What? How do you know what I'm wearing?" He chuckled, and although he never admitted it until years later, I knew he had put someone up to giving him a quick report as I walked into the building. His sense of humor was endearing, and put me totally at ease with his lack of sight.

That was the evening we went to the Hamburger Hamlet for dinner.

Now I know that Chris already told you about the catsup bottle, but this section is supposed to be in my words, so let me tell you the real story. We ordered our burgers and fries and I started eating. But not Chris. He started talking about *all of his life goals and business ambitions and the long and short-term objectives he mapped-out to reach them. He went on and on, and I was getting hungry and the burgers were getting cold. I reached for the catsup. I turned it upside down and shook it, but not wanting to interrupt Chris's discourse or distract him, I didn't pound on the bottom. That catsup would not budge, so I shook it harder and harder as Chris kept expounding on his plans. Finally, he interrupted my losing battle with the bottle by leaning forward and asking, "And what are your goals?"*

I calmly set the catsup bottle down and said, "Well, if you really want to know, my main goal in life is to get the catsup out of this bottle." Chris started laughing. He is so goal- oriented, while I am more concerned with the day-to-day events of life. We learned early on that we balance each other out perfectly.

***

As I got to know Chris better, I was even more amazed at his abilities. I'd be driving us somewhere and he'd mention that we should be passing a certain landmark. Once, I pulled out of a store parking lot, and Chris exclaimed, "Oh no, you're going the wrong way on a one-way street." Then all the drivers coming towards us started beeping their horns. Chris realized my error before I did. He knew the area around that store when he could see, but even in areas he had never seen, he was always asking his companions for descriptions and storing visual details in his mind.

He could do so many things, that often we'd meet people, and they would not immediately realize that Chris was blind. My older brother owned a gas station, and I told him about my new boyfriend. "I want you to meet this guy, but there is something about him that isn't right. I'll bring him by the station to meet you, and then you can give me your opinion." Later that day, Chris and I stopped at the station. As we walked into my brother's office, Chris stumbled a little on the threshold of the doorway, but quickly regained his balance. I introduced the two, and we had a short conversation. That night, I phoned my brother and asked what he thought of Chris.

"Oh, you can't fool me," he said, "that man has a wooden leg; I could tell by the way he was walking."

Yes, Chris Harvey was amazing, and I quickly fell in love with him.

15

Earthly Fatherhood — Playing It by Ear

*Which of you, if his son asks for bread
will give him a stone?
Or if he asks for a fish will give him a snake?
If you then, though you are evil, know how to give
good gifts to your children,
how much more will your Father in heaven give
good gifts to those who ask him.
Matthew 7:9-11*

"It's a boy!"

Chad Howell Harvey entered the world in the early morning of July 30, 1989. The doctor placed this warm and squirming fellow into my arms, and I held him long enough to count his fingers and toes before giving him to Stephanie. I had the phone numbers memorized and immediately started calling family and friends with the good news: "Chad is born. We have a son."

Blake Allen Harvey joined our family three years later. This mischievous bundle tricked me moments after he was born. When I held his tiny right hand, I could only feel a thumb. Trembling, I felt again, and was about to voice my concern when one of his little fingers popped up. Blake had his fingers curled up in such a tight fist that I didn't feel them. I gently dug into his palm and pried the other fingers up. One, two, three, four, five. "Thank you, Father God, thank you, thank you."

By the time our third child was born in 1994, I felt like an old pro in the labor and delivery arena. I knew all the coaching techniques to assist Stephanie, but I was surprised when the doctor asked, "Chris, if this is going to be your last baby, why don't you come around here and deliver it yourself?"

"Really?" Did this obstetrician actually trust a blind man to deliver a baby on his watch?

"Scrub up and put on a gown and some gloves."

"Yes sir." My voice sounded more confident than I felt. One of the nurses got me suited up, and the next thing I knew, the doc was placing my hands on the baby's crowning head.

"Here, support the head with your left hand." He then took my right hand and placed it on a little arm that had emerged. "Grip the shoulder from under the arm pit."

As the second arm slipped out, the doctor grasped it and took hold of the chest. "On three, we're pulling, okay? Keep holding as I showed you."

I remember going through the motions as instructed, but I think I was in shock as I helped bring our third child into the world. I barely heard the count, but pulled on "Three." I was surprised at how quickly the baby slipped out, but the bigger surprise came when the doctor announced, "It's a girl."

"A girl?" For nine months, I assumed that we'd have another boy and raise three rambunctious sons. "A girl? Are you sure, doc?"

Before the doctor could figure out how to answer that one, the foolishness of my question hit me, and I blurted out, "Of course you're sure. You've done this a few times, haven't you?" We all had a good laugh before the nurse handed me our daughter, Victoria Jean Harvey. My rambunctious third "son" immediately became the princess that stole her daddy's heart.

***

My whole perspective on life changed as I witnessed the miracle of birth. I felt such closeness to God and realized that my joy was a small reflection of the joy God must feel when another of his children is reborn.

I remember Chad's head tucked under my chin like a softball when he was a few days old. His tiny little fingers, toes, kneecaps, and elbows thrilled me. I'd cradle him in the crook of my elbow like a fresh loaf of bread—a compact little miracle of God's love, full and complete. Each of our newborns was a precious gift from God, and I wanted to be the best father possible.

If I harbored any thoughts of using my lack of sight to get out of the less pleasant baby tasks, I kept them to myself. Stephanie always encouraged my desire to be an involved father—even in those areas that I could have completely delegated to her.

For instance, I was no stranger to changing diapers—mostly wet ones, but messy ones when that was needed, too. When I did have to attack a messy diaper, I'd tend to clean the baby from one end to the other, using a whole stack of diaper wipes. I wanted to be sure that I didn't miss anything. The little guys probably appreciated their mother's abbreviated version of clean-up.

When Chad was nearly a year old, Stephanie took a part-time evening and weekend job. I supported her decision, and felt it was a great opportunity for her to get out of the house. Others looked at it differently, though. Several friends wondered how she could leave her infant at home with a blind father. This act of trust on Stephanie's part demonstrated one of her greatest traits: she has a tender, protective side, but she is also tough enough to let me do what we both know that I'm capable of handling.

As the popular saying goes, Stephanie didn't "sweat the small stuff." She gave me the freedom to take responsibility, and never mentioned those things that I did that may not have met her standards. It is so important that Stephanie expected me to do a lot, despite my disability. I would not have wanted her to coddle me into a handicapped dad on the sidelines of my kids' lives. Stephanie's expectations helped me to rise and become the capable man I am today. It takes a strong mother to trust a blind father with her baby, and sometimes I did make mistakes.

One evening I was home alone with Chad and he was having a terrible time teething. As I held my crying son on my left shoulder, I groped around for the "gum numb" on the kitchen counter. I located the small bottle, unscrewed the top, doused my fingertip with the liquid, and gently rubbed it on Chad's gums. He immediately stopped screaming. "Like that, little buddy? How about some more?" I proceeded to coat his upper and lower gums, and he snuggled down into my arms.

When Stephanie got home from work, I held up the bottle and said, "This stuff sure works great." As it turned out, I'd soothed the baby with almond extract.

Another time, I woke up early with a stuffy nose and made the coffee before Stephanie and Chad awoke. I enjoyed my first cup, and then poured myself another and one for Stephanie. *She'll really appreciate my thoughtfulness—coffee in bed.* I placed the steaming cup on her bedside table and made my way to the bathroom to get ready for work. Stephanie muttered, "What *is* this?"

"It's coffee. Pretty good, huh? I'm on my second cup."

"Chris, this can't be coffee," she retorted, "it's white and foamy."

It turned out that the can of powdered baby formula was sitting adjacent to the coffee can, and they were similar in size and shape. I'd obviously grabbed the wrong one and brewed up some formula instead. My nose was so stuffy that I couldn't taste the difference—I'd actually thought it was quite good. The funniest part was that Stephanie discovered little "pancakes" were forming on the warming tray of the coffee maker, where the formula dripped when the pot was removed. We still laugh about those formula pancakes. At least I didn't give Chad a bottle of coffee.

***

Things became tricky when our infants began to crawl, though. With the three children born within five years, we had little ones underfoot for quite a while. As long as they made some sort of noise for me to follow, I was able to "watch out" for them. Collisions were sometimes unavoidable, though, when a curious toddler was quietly preoccupied. In fact, they quickly learned to get out of my way after being bumped over or jostled by being in my path.

As our children became walkers, they learned to look for Daddy as much as Daddy was listening for them. It is amazing that none of them ever became "road-kill" from my lumbering over, on, or through them. Maybe side view mirrors would have helped them to see Daddy coming.

They also learned the hard way to keep their toys off the floor, or at least out of the traffic-ways. I stepped on and broke many toys, which made me feel terrible. Sometimes replacing the toy remedied the loss for the kids. Other times, the toy was not replaceable. They learned to get over these losses and move on—and they acquired the habit of putting their things away a little earlier in life than they might have otherwise.

Stephanie was home most of the time when the children were small, so my total responsibility was limited. However, with her part-time jobs, housekeeping chores, and errands to run, I had my share of supervising. At times, it was a challenge to listen to where they were and what they were each doing. I had to anticipate which direction they were going next, and what they might be attracted to. Even a sighted dad watching three young children has a difficult time. We did all that we could to childproof the rooms, but sometimes that doesn't work—whether you can see the little rascals or not. Nevertheless, I kept up with them well enough to protect them from significant harm, thank you, Jesus.

Hopefully, having a blind daddy made my children more observant and aware of their circumstances than other children might be. However, to this day (and they are teens now) they still occasionally forget that they need to look out for me or warn me of obstacles. It is perhaps the greatest compliment I could receive, when my own family members forget for a second that I can't see.

***

But for all the joy of fatherhood, the pain of not seeing my children is unavoidable. I can't deny the fact that I feel deprived to never see their smiling faces or look into their eyes. I can't dwell on that though, and God showed me that I could still find joy in experiencing my children through touch and sound. By holding my babies and listening to their gurgles, coos, and even their cries, I was able to develop mental images of them. I could not wait for them to start talking and communicate with me. When I think back, or when we watch old family videos, their tiny little voices still thrill me.

I also have wonderful memories of the children modeling behaviors after their daddy. When I pour milk into my glass, I place my finger inside the rim to alert me when the liquid is nearing the top. Around the ages of three to five, Stephanie noticed that the children placed a finger inside the rim of their cups—the same as daddy did. They weren't sure why they did it, since they hadn't grasped my need to know the cup is full without seeing it fill up. Such occurrences were so precious, and reinforced to me how much children watch their parents and automatically learn about life from them. I try to remember that my example continues to influence my children, no matter how old they are. Although I can't set a perfect example like the one our Father in heaven does, I need to aim toward that goal.

***

Beyond the heartbreak of not being able to see my children, my limited ability to interact with them is my second greatest disappointment as a blind father. When I think of my own childhood, I remember special times with my dad. I'd always looked up to him as a businessman, and wanted to grow up to be like him, carrying a briefcase and wearing a suit to work. But there was another side to my dad that I'll never forget: work ended at the door of our house. When he was at home, his attentions were towards his family. Whether we were working in the yard together or doing a jigsaw puzzle, Dad was there for us.

He was a member of the Rocky Gorge Gun Club, and would take my brother, Craig, and me with him to target shoot and to hunt in season. I have great memories of camping with Dad and Craig in my uncle's tiny one-axle camping trailer—we once all stepped to the back of the trailer, causing it to flip up on one end. We still laugh about that adventure and the fun times fishing in our little Jon Boat (which Craig accidentally punctured with his archery set—but that's another story), or camping in a rented pop-up trailer.

Dad was also involved with my little league teams, and he and Mom were always in the stands when I played football, baseball, and lacrosse. I realize now how much security and encouragement I felt knowing they were there. One of my greatest prayers is that even when I can't participate fully in their activities, my children will always know that I am there for them.

***

Chad is an extremely talented drummer and I love to hear him play, but it would also be nice to watch the blur of drumsticks in his hands and the steady beat of his foot on the bass pedal. Blake is hooked on skate boarding, plays the guitar, and is our resident technical and mechanical genius. Tori is a gifted dancer. I love to hear the music and imagine her movement as she dances on the stage, but wish I could truly watch her performances. Even more than watching any of them in their special activities, I'd just like to have the opportunity to see their smiles.

Please don't misunderstand me; I am grateful for the interactions we are still able to enjoy. I have thrown the football to the kids for years now. As my young receivers, they tried to catch a wide variety of trajectories, sharpening their skills. "We're gonna go long, so let 'er rip," they might whisper to me before taking a stance.

"On two." I would whisper back, and then, "Hut, hut." Little feet scampered away through the grass and I would let the sound fade a little before passing the ball.

"Whoa," they would exclaim, as the ball fired up into the air.

"Run to it," I would shout, and then turn around to pretend I couldn't bear to watch as they crashed into each other trying to claim the catch.

And then there is basketball. The kids have always been patient with me while I try repeatedly to shoot baskets from the imaginary foul line. They take shots to help me hear where the basket is and then hand me the ball. "Short," they cry out as the ball falls silently to the ground. Or, "Over," when it clears the backboard entirely and I exclaim like Bullwinkle, "Sometimes I don't know my own strength."

Finally, a jubilant swish and the chink of the chains let me know I made a basket. Often I can zone-in for two or even three baskets in a row when I am "sighted in." After a little success, I have to bow out; I am embarrassed to say, so my elbows won't hurt the next day.

When the kids were in elementary school, we lived in a house with a swimming pool and created fun with "projectile swimming" meets. There were two styles of projectile swimming. In the first version, the kids would float into place with their backs to me and stand on my bent knees. I would hold them under their armpits and bounce three times. "One" I would call out with the first bounce. "Two" with the second bounce, which usually drew a laugh or shriek. "Three," and they would take a deep breath as I used our momentum to toss them up into the air, so they could plunge into the deep end of the pool.

The second version of projectile swimming was the more popular request. This time the young swimmer would again swim up to me, but this time in the middle of the pool. Positioned where the floor began to drop toward the deep end, I would cramp down under the water's surface. The floating youngster who had been holding on to my shoulders before I submerged would then paddle forward and position one foot on each of my shoulders. When firmly in place for a second or so, I would spring up from the bottom. We got good at our timing, and the kids could fly high into the air and dive into the deep end. As they got older, they were even able to get enough height to do a flip.

It wouldn't be fair to keep all of this fun for ourselves, so we invited the neighborhood kids to participate, with their parents' permission. Soon there were nearly daily projectile swimming meets in our back yard throughout the summer.

"That's one thing Dad does that other dads don't do," my kids would proudly exclaim.

I can't do other things, however. If I could drive, I could give Stephanie a break and take the children to their music or dance lessons, or take them on errands to have the one-on-one time we rarely get. I can't coach their sports or umpire Little League Baseball, as I had always dreamed I would do, but instead I cheer them on from the sidelines. Although my presence is important to them, it would be more gratifying to both them and me if I could see what they do. My relationship with each of them would be another level deeper or intimate if I could see everything they saw, to discuss with them. I could do so much more with them if I still had the sight I was born with.

There are still hugs, clicking our fingers before high fiveing each other, and Tori and I share butterfly kisses each night before bed. But they have to grow up with a father who is limited in what he can do to lead his family in earthly activities.

***

I enjoy being the spiritual head of my family because I love the Lord and look forward to corporately worshiping him each week. One time, when Tori was in elementary school, Stephanie had to be away for the weekend. On that Sunday morning, Tori asked why we didn't skip church and sleep in, since Stephanie was not there to drive us. Tori's question made sense. It would be easier to stay home than to find a ride to church, but I turned and said, "I want to go to church so I can learn more about God and worship him with everybody." To which Tori replied, "Oh, okay." She giggled and ran up the steps.

I remember my own father's witness about right and wrong when I was about twelve years old. We were squirrel hunting, and he reminded me to stay on one side of the dirt road because there were "no trespassing" signs posted on the other side. Seeing squirrels by the dozens on the "no trespassing" side of the fence as we walked the old dirt road drove me crazy. "But Dad, look! There are millions of them over there!" His response was gentle, but firm in telling me that was the law. I remember harboring critical thoughts about Dad's inflexibility on even the tiniest of violations. As I grew into adulthood, I realized how strong a man Dad was. His adherence to what is clearly right and avoiding what is clearly wrong is a moral standard that I still aspire to. His own actions communicated even stronger than the words he spoke.

I hope that over time, my actions and words guide my children in the right direction in life, toward having a relationship with God through Jesus. The Bible says that God doesn't desire our offerings and sacrifices, but instead wants us to have an attitude of justice and mercy and to have a relationship with him. Micah 6:7-9 says, "He has showed you, O man, what is good. And what does the LORD require of you? To act justly and to love mercy and to walk humbly with your God." I try to act justly and love mercy in my dealings with others, and to walk humbly with God.

In addition to my outward witness, I strive for a silent witness through the fruit of the spirit, listed in Galatians 5:22-23: love, joy, peace, patience, kindness, goodness, gentleness, faithfulness, and self-control. When my heart and life reflect these virtues, my children will be touched and feel loved because of it.

***

My reward as an earthly father has been to have three loving children. I know how I feel about them—I love them unconditionally and only want the best for them. Stephanie and I have always made family a priority. We constantly strive to provide a good model for our children, and to teach them responsibility and honesty. But they are individuals, and they have to make choices. As they face the teenage years, I find that communication with them can be challenging. I'm sure that God is trying to teach me something as I work through these struggles to communicate well in certain areas. I have to be open to God's instruction and rely on the fruit of the Spirit to nurture and maintain communication with my teens—and with every other relationship.

Sometimes I wonder how God must feel about me as his child. I know he wants to protect me from harm. Yet he made man with a free will, so my own choices often bring adversity into my life. God is able to take that adversity and help me to learn from it. I'd give anything to keep my own children from harm, but I must allow them to make mistakes. That doesn't keep me from feeling frustrated when they make a wrong choice, so I can only imagine how frustrated God gets with me. Praise God, he is always there to forgive me and cradle me in his arms of protection. My rejoicing in my children's triumphs and sharing in their troubles is merely a glimpse into the magnitude with which God celebrates and comforts me throughout my journey on earth. I aspire to make sure each of my kids knows they are loved, and that I am always available for them. What else can an earthly father do to demonstrate our Lord's love for all of us?

Part Two:

Reflections on a Life without Sight

16

Stepping onto the Stage

"For I know the plans I have for you,"
declares the LORD,
"plans to prosper you and not to harm you,
plans to give you hope and a future."
Jeremiah 29:11

Accepting my future without sight was like being handed an unfamiliar script and then being pushed onto stage with hardly more than a "get on out there, you're on."

I have done some acting since that time of my life, and looking back, I realize that my initial performance as a blind person consisted of improvisation and prayer. The audience may think that the role of the actor is easy because those on stage appear flawless and carry themselves smoothly in the spotlight. What appears effortless is due to weeks of study and rehearsal, though. The role of a blind man was not what I had rehearsed for my life. I didn't want to be in any spotlight, but I had to choose to perform in this role, or take a permanent seat in the dark shadows of self-pity.

Most of us would rather sit in the audience than perform, and I am no different. Stage fright can be immobilizing. The thought of seizing up or failing as a blind man was intimidating to me. When I could see, I always enjoyed and excelled at team sports. In high school, I was the All-County defensive tackle on our championship football team. I also played baseball and lacrosse, all team sports that we won or lost as a group. I loved to watch wrestling, but I never chose to compete in it because of the risk of individual embarrassment.

After losing my sight, I felt like the wrestler defending his dignity on the mat, or the lone actor on the stage. I imagined the eyes of friends and fellow students upon me wherever I went. Their comments demonstrated that my imagination was not far from the truth. People spoke up unexpectedly about something they thought I was about to do, or something they thought I should know. Yes, others were watching my every move. For example, a well-meaning person might shove a napkin at me, or comment on the size of the piece of lettuce on my fork. Out of concern or out of curiosity, people watched me like never before. My blindness acted like a spotlight that kept all eyes focused on me, while not allowing me to see out into the darkened audience.

Even after years of blindness, I still must deal with this spotlight phenomenon. For example, people see me from a distance, and by the time they have gotten close to me, they already have a greeting or remark to make. Since I've had no warning of their presence until they speak, I have only a second or two to determine who they are (even familiar voices may be difficult to identify in a noisy environment) and to formulate my response.

In addition, there are always jokesters in the crowd. I love a good joke, but coming up to a blind person and playing the "guess who?" game is not funny. One acquaintance seemed to think I was a carnival sideshow and announced to others present, "Hey, get a load of this. I cleared my throat and Chris knew who it was." Now really, I knew this clown was in the group, and he was the best guess as to who would tease me. I try to remain cheerful, but what is a game to these people is my day-to-day life.

Another uncomfortable situation occurs when a person approaches me and grasps my arm to get my attention, but then doesn't say anything, as if I am supposed to recognize them. Again, I realize the person means no harm, but it does put me in an awkward position.

I've also noticed over the years that whenever I walk into a room of people, everyone wants me to sit down. Why do people always want the blind guy to sit, especially when many of them are standing and mingling? Even the ladies pop up and offer me their chairs. My usual response is to say, "I sit for a living, so it feels good to stand."

Another thing I encounter is that people tend to speak loudly when they are addressing me, as if my lack of sight causes my hearing to decrease. When this is obvious enough to be uncomfortable, I may say, "Easy now. I'm blind, not deaf."

And in restaurants, the wait staff often assumes that I am deaf as well as blind. Once at breakfast, a waitress turned to my friend and asked, "How does he want his eggs cooked?"

I replied, "He likes them over easy."

***

I know that these well-meaning friends and acquaintances are seeking their own comfort level in the presence of the blind man. But really, I'm a regular old person, and I'm not shy about asking if I do need help. Of course, if I'm about to endanger myself or someone else, I do appreciate a warning from my friends. I guess I'd like to be treated as normal as possible. The best advice I can give when being around a blind person is to "relax."

Fortunately, I had a good sense of humor before losing my sight, and this has served me well in dealing with these uncomfortable situations. And when I am able to laugh at myself, everyone around me feels more comfortable. A funny remark can spare us all embarrassment when someone has made an inappropriate remark, or when I do something clumsy. For example, when I'm moving through a crowded area, holding the arm of someone, it's easy for me to bump into others, so I warn, "Wide load coming through," or "I'm a big guy and I make a large sidecar." This clears my pathway with everyone smiling.

***

I had to make a critical choice in handling the spotlight of blindness. I could have dropped out of my college fraternity, avoided the cafeteria and local restaurants, and become a semi-recluse, only going to classes. I could have avoided noisy social situations where it was difficult to communicate. And I probably would have never gone on to graduate school.

Thankfully, God made me both an over-achiever and an extrovert, and he gave me parents who encouraged me never to give up. As it says in Ephesians 1:4-6, "Long ago, before God laid down the earth's foundations, he had settled on us as the focus of his love, to be made whole and holy by his love." I am so fortunate that God knew the visual challenge I would face in life and built me to deal with it. I knew what my choice would be. I would accept the role and step onto that stage and into the spotlight. What I didn't immediately realize is that no actor is alone in the spotlight. There are technical people working behind the scenes, there are supporting actors, and of course, there is the director.

At the time I lost my sight, I was at the developmental level of seeking and proving my independence. This milestone is important, since it prepares young people to be self-sufficient, responsible citizens; however, it's not the last level of maturation.

Blindness forced me to make the transition from independence back to dependence instantly — and I have to admit, involuntarily. In my youthful pride, I thought that I was very self-sufficient, but I was thrust into needing others for my routine existence.

There were the obvious areas of need, like transportation, cleaning, coordinating my clothing, shopping for and preparing my meals, and reading things to me. But I found that I also needed emotional support. I needed the encouragement of my family and friends to keep me going when all seemed uphill. I needed the security that my family and friends would help meet my needs as I learned how to do things without sight. As a result, stepping onto the stage required that I trade my pride for humility.

***

When I realized that needing others was not a sign of weakness, nor did it mean that I could not contribute to their lives, I took a major step towards accepting the bounds of blindness. As I learned skills to compensate for lack of sight, much of my self-sufficiency returned. In my youthful mindset, though, total independence was necessary to prove my maturity. God used my blindness to teach me interdependence, the merging of dependence and independence in human relationships. Some people take longer than others do in making the transition to interdependence in their lives. The desire for independence may make them too prideful to accept or even think they need help from others. Ultimately, man is not meant to be alone. Our relationships with God and with others are more important than anything else is on earth. Helping others and allowing them to help you when you are in need is what relationships are all about. And I've learned that accepting help from others makes them more comfortable about accepting help from me.

The greatest lesson, though, was when I understood that God was my director on the stage of life, and he held the script for the future. My life, with or without sight, is completely dependent on God. When I trust him with the script, I can step onto that stage of blindness with confidence—not in my own self-sufficiency, but in total dependence on my creator.

When the bullet struck me, I instinctively knew that God was in charge. I had no choice but to totally trust him. Even if I did not understand the plans he had for me, I knew that he loved me and would never harm me. I firmly believed (and still believe) that God spared my life and kept the impact of the disaster to a minimum. His quiet voice calmed me and assured me that I would still reach the potential that he had created in me even before my birth. But, I had to hand him back the script that I'd envisioned for my life. He became my director, the one I still look to every morning for help in living my life, not just as a blind man, but also as a child of God. I chose to take up my new role. I had to step back onto the stage of life in the spotlight of my disability. With God's help, I wanted to give my tragedy purpose. I chose to walk by faith and not by sight.

17

Life with Four Senses

*And if your eye causes you to sin, pluck it out.
It is better for you to enter the kingdom of God with
one eye than have two eyes and be thrown into hell.*
Mark 9:47

With one good eye, I'd still have all of my independence. It would have been a luxury to lose only one eye as in Christ's axiom. Yet, when I read Jesus' words in Mark, I remind myself that maybe I should be twice as grateful as the person who only lost one eye, that I am not going to hell.

Perhaps I would have been twice as big a sinner if I'd had even one eye. Maybe I would have led an uninspired life, more concerned with my own success in business and the mighty dollar, if I had never lost my sight. I may not totally understand God's plan, but in Jeremiah 29:11, God promises that he has a plan for my life, a plan not to harm me, but to give me hope and a future, so who am I to question why I lost both eyes?

In his perfect plan, though, God created man with five senses—sight, hearing, touch, smell, and taste. The brain uses input from each sense to provide a composite impression about the environment. When a person loses one or more of the senses, he must learn to rely on those that remain. I still have my hearing, touch, taste, and smell to provide me with information about my surroundings, and I thank God for those blessings. When I think that I could have been paralyzed or severely brain-damaged and on life-support for decades, only being blinded from the gunshot wound does not seem so bad. In fact, being "only blinded" was, and continues to be, an answer to my prayer in the helicopter.

***

People often ask me if I'd rather be blind or deaf. It is impossible to answer such a question. I am content that being blind is not more difficult than being deaf, but is rather a different kind of difficult.

Because several family members experienced hearing loss as they grew older, I do fear the loss of my hearing—the sense that I rely on to gather most of my information. Being the jokester that I am, I tease that my name will be Harvey

Keller if I also lose my hearing. I say that with great admiration for Helen Keller, and wonder how she managed her life.

Hearing is a tremendous bridge to knowing and embracing my family. Stephanie is my closest friend and soul mate, and our conversations are precious to me. The children's voices fill me with joy, and through conversations with them, I'm able to share in their lives. Besides that, heaven knows they probably get away with enough mischief that I can't see. I wouldn't even want to think about what they might try to pull if I couldn't hear them.

I praise God for preserving my hearing, and I love to hear the crackling of a fire, the chirp of a cricket, or the symphony of the katydids that roll in waves across the woods behind my house. I can't see the graceful flight of a bird, but I can hear the coo and the whoosh of wings as a pair of doves takes flight near me—and I've even perfected my dove call to where doves on my hillside answer me.

I am fortunate to be able to enjoy music. It's amazing how sounds can affect our moods and influence our dispositions. Music takes me back to the 1960s and 1970s when I had my sight, and prompts visual memories. Music has the ability to charge me up or chill me out. And, no matter how many times I've heard our National Anthem, I still nearly burst my shirt buttons with pride when I hear it. Music also brings me to worship. Old hymns, like "How Great Thou Art" and "Amazing Grace," can bring tears to my eyes—

yes, even my artificial eyes. The splendor of connecting with God through song is awesome, and I often feel caught up in his presence through the music.

***

While hearing brings me pleasure, it also serves as my primary alert system and source of information for decision-making. Imagine a business situation where you and a peer must solve the same problem. The peer has access to all of the research to reach the best decision; however, you receive only part of the information. Without sight, I must make my decisions with less information than those around me. I am able to do so, but the process requires more effort and is more stressful for me.

As a simple example, I try to determine who walked into the room by the sounds they make. Even when my own family members come downstairs, I have to try to guess who it is when they don't speak by how heavy they walk, or by the tone of their humming, singing, or even clearing their throat. When I walk through my home, I must listen for the sounds of others to avoid a collision. Although I might hear my wife drop a utensil into the sink, she may turn sharply to head in the opposite direction of what I had guessed. And the kids are probably even more unpredictable. It was much easier to know where they were when I was able to put jingle bells on their baby shoes, and could hear the crinkle of their little diapers as they moved around. You can't "sound alarm" all those around you, though.

I rely on environmental sounds as well as human sounds. The opening of a door, the hum of the refrigerator, the honking of a horn, the whir of a lawnmower, and all of the sounds my computer makes create a mental image of what is going on around me.

Nearly everyone asks me the same question when we first meet. They have heard that the other senses become more acute when one is lost. They always want to know if sounds amplify when you can't see. My favorite response is, "I don't hear dog whistles in Alaska, if that's what you mean." It is not as though my eardrums developed their own hearing aids and turned up the volume. But over a period, I did become more in tune to sounds after I lost my sight. This is not a phenomenon, but is the result of my learning to pay closer attention to the auditory stimuli around me.

I almost have to chuckle that other people think my hearing decreased when I lost my sight, and they speak loudly around me. I intentionally speak more softly to encourage them to tone it down. When the person is a friend, I can tease, "All right already. I'm blind, not deaf. "

The truth of the matter is that I use my hearing differently to absorb my environment. For instance, many times I realize someone has entered the room before my sighted companions are aware of the visitor. I might hear the doorknob turn or the visitor sniff or clear his throat well before the others, caught up in conversation, turn to observe who walked in. And I'm usually more aware of objects falling to the floor or objects slid across a table when others are visually distracted.

***

Do you remember the "Feely Bag" game from kindergarten, where you place your hand into a bag and identify objects by feel? That is how I use my sense of touch to identify objects in my environment. Putting away groceries is a good example of what I call my "safari of tactile observance," as I sort cans, boxes, veggies, fruits, and meats after a trip to the grocery store. My tactile sense stimulates my brain and I can visualize the objects in near perfect 3-D. Specific cans and boxes are a little more difficult to identify, but often can be recognized by size or sound. A pudding box is one size, while macaroni is another. My sense of hearing adds more information as the pasta rattles in the macaroni box.

Unlike my sense of hearing, my sense of touch seemed to intensify since losing my sight—or perhaps it's that my perspective has changed as I've learned to rely on this sense more. Objects now feel larger than they used to look. I first noticed this change when I hugged others. Friends and family all felt larger in my clutches than I recalled them looking. An object like a hair dryer sitting on a countertop used to look relatively small and insignificant. Now, when I lift it off the counter and feel the weight, it appears heavier and larger than I remember it visually.

Besides weight and size, my touch also alerts me to textures that I probably would have never noticed when I had my sight. One day I was making hamburger patties for the grill. As I finished one container of ground beef and started on the second one, I commented that the meat felt coarser and less greasy. It turned out that the second container had a 5 percent lower fat content.

I am reminded of the fairy tale, "The Princess and the Pea," when I describe this phenomenon. When the princess tried to lie down on a stack of mattresses, she could still feel the pea under the bottom of the stack. The smallest of imperfections had its ripple effect all the way to the top, and the smallest of bumps bothered the sensitive maiden. I can identify with her. It bothers me to lie on the top sheet in bed, because even the smallest wrinkle in it bugs me. I pay such attention to tactile details, that I can feel a single strand of hair or grain of sand or soil on a smooth surface like a countertop. I still like the beach, but now sand in my chair, on the floor, in my bed, or other places, absolutely drives me nuts.

***

Touch does give me valuable information, but touch is not a good warning system. One time, a friend dropped me off at home. I entered the kitchen door and, before placing the bag I was carrying on the kitchen counter, I swept my hand across the surface to be sure it was clear. Stephanie had stepped out of the kitchen just before I walked in, and was unable to warn me about the hard candy she had just poured into cookie sheets on the counter. The fingers of my left hand landed in the molten concoction. Stephanie called 911 and they instructed us to place my hand under running water to cool the candy down as quickly as possible. As the chunks of candy fell from my fingers, the second- and third-degree burns revealed themselves. Wrapping my hand in a cold, wet dishtowel, we were off to the emergency room for first aid and pain medicine.

This episode is an extreme example, but shows that touch is not a reliable warning system. I have dents in my shins from finding coffee tables and seats of chairs unexpectedly. My toes are stubbed, cut, and bruised from hitting furniture, partially open doors, and the bottoms of kitchen cabinets with bare feet. I have been stubborn about wearing shoes around the house because I like to let my "dogs breathe," as I call it. After wearing dress shoes all day and athletic shoes to exercise, it is refreshing for my feet to be bare. The fact of the matter is that I should probably wear steel-tipped boots everywhere I go.

Fortunately, my sense of touch also provides pleasure. Stephanie's caress and our children's hugs are two examples of pleasure that I do not have to see to experience. A shoulder or backrub, holding hands, or massage therapy have their benefits whether you can see or not. Jesus often touched people to comfort or to heal them, and he even washed the feet of his disciples—a tender demonstration of serving people through touch.

***

My senses of taste and smell are closely related, and can soothe me or warn me of danger. The gunshot wound that took my sight also caused temporary damage to my sinuses. For several months following the shooting, I experienced a diminished sense of smell, which affected my taste reception. Even peanut butter was tasteless when I could not smell it. As I healed from my injuries, my senses of smell and taste returned. This experience taught me how important the aromas of different foods are to provide the pleasure that comes from eating.

My sense of smell can serve to warn me as well. I can tell if a restroom is unsanitary and proceed cautiously. I can smell mold, which is good since I have an acute allergy to it.

Certain smells or memories of smells enhance my mental picture. That aroma from a Thanksgiving dinner cooking brings fond memories of family gatherings growing up. New York City conjures up aromas of old-fashioned Italian restaurants I have visited over my lifetime. And, fresh popped popcorn either means you are at the movies or Wal-Mart.

***

Before losing my sight, I never realized how much information we relay and receive through our eyes, our facial expressions, and even how we stand, hold our arms, or position ourselves in physical relationship to others while talking. Research shows that human communication is 80 percent nonverbal. Without sight, I do not receive this nonverbal information from others, and must pay closer attention to my own body language as well. For example, think about how often you have a serious look on your face, but when you see someone approaching, you're all peaches and cream by the time they get close to you. I try to maintain a pleasant expression—because I am not aware of others approaching me until they've had a chance to see my face.

So how do I manage to gain information that I can't see? Every situation I encounter as a blind man begins with a blank slate. Let me explain. Suppose you notice a friend walking towards you. You see that he is wearing casual clothes, has a bag from the local sports store in his left hand, and a huge fountain soda in his right hand. Through the translucent bag, you can faintly make out the words "Golf Balls" on a box. Before the friend speaks, you already know who is present, what he's wearing, where he shopped, and you might even assume that he's headed to the golf course.

With the same situation, I would not know who approached me until the person spoke and I recognized his voice, or he identified himself. I would not know what he was wearing. I'd have no clue that he had been shopping in general, or specifically at a sports store.

When I realize who the person is, I place him on my mental slate. As he shakes my hand, I notice that his hand is cold and damp. This unexpected information goes onto the slate. When he apologizes for the clammy hand and tells me he was holding a soda, I understand. When he sets his bag down, I note the crinkle of the plastic and the dull thud of the object in the bag contacting the floor. I add "bag and something with weight" to my mental slate, but until he mentions that he's recently taken up golf, and that he's lost so many balls that he had to buy more, I have no clue to the contents. (And when he says he is on his way to the golf course, I understand why his aftershave smells like bug spray.)

Piece by piece, my senses help me complete the puzzle on my mental slate. I appreciate my ability to hear, smell, touch, and taste, and I am thankful for twenty years of sight. Because I have visual images in my memory, I have an easier time filling in the missing pieces on my slate—maybe not with perfect information, but with enough to give me closure. Thank you, Lord Jesus.

18

Built for this World

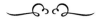

*Long before he laid down the earth's foundation,
he had settled upon us as the focus of His love,
to be made whole and holy by His love.
Long, long ago he decided to adopt us into his
family through Jesus Christ.
(What pleasure he took in planning this.)
Ephesians 1:4 The Message*

Sometimes people tend to view those with disabilities as less than whole, but in God's eyes, I am both whole and holy. Even before he created the world, God had me in his mind, and through the sacrifice of his son Jesus, adopted me into the family of God.

God didn't only do that for me, but for every person born into this world. Even before conception, God made us the focus of his love. He knew our future, and he created us with strengths and talents to cope with our circumstances.

I am sure that God prepared me emotionally for a life of blindness while I was still a child. Beyond that, he created me with natural abilities and he provided learning opportunities that have helped me to cope with the loss of my sight. New challenges arise daily, and I am able to meet them. This is neither my own doing nor my own strength, but a gift from the loving Father. He created my personality and gave me mental and physical talents to face whatever my circumstances are in life. My responsibility is to be a good steward of these gifts and use them first to God's glory, and in doing so, to become the person he intended for me to be.

Although we have different talents and abilities, there is one gift that we all have equal access to, the gift of the Holy Spirit. Before his death, Jesus told his disciples that he would be going away, but that he would send a comforter to dwell within each of them. As the Spirit of God filled the disciples, the Spirit also dwells within us, standing in the gap when our natural abilities fall short, leading us closer to the heart of God, and giving us wisdom when we are at our weakest. By depending on the Holy Spirit to help me through every day, I am able to better use the natural talents that God has given me, as well.

Somehow, knowing that God built me for this world makes it a little easier to find peace and hope in my journey here on earth. Although one of my first job interviewers in the financial field felt that no one could be a stockbroker without vision, I've found that God perfectly suited me for this job.

***

First, God built me with a good memory. The more I memorize, the less work I have to do. Let me explain. Even though I have a talking database on my computer, it takes time to scroll through records, listening to an electronic voice. By God's grace, I am able to remember hundreds of phone numbers and even client account numbers. I can usually recall details of transactions, including dates and purchase prices. God gave me a mind that can comprehend, sort, store, and retrieve information without seeing any of it. Clients often remark about my memory, to which I can only say, "To God be the glory for making me this way."

When I was in the process of applying to different graduate schools, the dean at the University of Virginia warned my father that a blind person would not be able to handle the three-dimensional graphs that were integral to the economics coursework. By God's divine grace, I was able to visualize those graphs from verbal descriptions. Likewise, in my career as a stockbroker, I am able to visualize two-dimensional graphs of the technical patterns of individual stocks.

I can generally track the moving average prices for some stocks and indexes in my head. Fellow brokers are amazed when I guess on the money, or only off by a point or two, for the one-year moving average price. (The one-year or two-hundred-day average price of a stock or index is a mathematical guideline in our industry.) I tend to develop a feel for how much a stock has been progressing or declining over time with casual daily price observations, and a mental library that keeps track of moving data.

God built these mathematical abilities into me before I was even born. I knew I'd have a career that involved mathematics, in either the business world or possibly teaching economics on the college level. But I never considered a career as a stockbroker. In his perfect wisdom, God opened doors of opportunity for an investment career that has proven to be perfectly suited for a man without sight.

***

My love of the business world and finance began when I was a young child. Whether this was my nature, or the nurture of my businessman father, I don't know. Either way, God used my childhood as a training ground for business skills that I depend on daily as an adult.

One of my early memories is of getting an allowance. I loved to hold and sort the coins and arrange dollars in my little rawhide wallet. As a blind adult, I also sort and arrange the currency in my wallet so that I know what denomination bill I'm handing a clerk. My childhood piggy bank resembled a safe and was the recipient of my savings until I was about seven years old. At that time, I opened a passbook bank account. As I entered the deposits into my passbook, I dreamed of the possibilities. In fact, when I first heard the word *economist,* I thought I should grow up to be one since I was already doing a good job of economizing. I was frugal in my spending so that I could continue to add to my savings. I remember thinking I was well on my way to one hundred dollars when my balance crossed the thirty-dollar level. And when I reached one hundred dollars, I'd be on the way to one thousand dollars.

My dad was my hero. He watched the news each evening, and even if I was playing with my toys, I listened to the broadcasts along with him. He also read newspapers daily, so I quickly learned the importance and the impact of the world outside of my family. I watched Dad leave for work each morning, wearing his suit and tie and carrying a briefcase, and I wanted to be like him when I grew up. One of my greatest memories was of a Saturday when he took me to the office with him. He worked for 3M Corporation, in an office building on Pennsylvania Avenue in downtown Washington, D.C. While he worked, I kept busy with drawing pictures, but I also spent a lot of time looking around. I loved everything about the office. There were desks and typewriters, filing cabinets, and massive tape recorders used by NASA. I relished the smells —the typewriter oil, the paper products, the furniture polish, and even the aroma of new carpet. I was mystified when I looked out the windows of this tall building and found myself peering into the windows of other tall buildings. The magical environment of business left me awestruck.

At age ten, I started my own business. Lemonade stands didn't interest me, so I developed a tie-dye company in the basement of our home. Mom took me to the supermarket where I selected five colors of fabric dye. My customers were to supply their own tee shirts, and they could choose from blue, red, yellow, green, or orange dyes. I started at one dollar and fifty cents for one color; additional colors were fifty cents each. I took orders during the day, tie-dyed after supper, and delivered the finished product the next day. This business boomed at first, but I quickly learned a basic concept of marketing—the need for a wide customer base. My marketing region was limited to the neighborhood, so I'd soon exhausted all of the available customers.

When the tie-dye business waned, I helped a friend deliver the *Washington Post*. I then obtained my own route delivering the *Prince George County Sentinel* on my ten-speed bike. I remember my excitement over the new construction of the Calverton Apartments—when people started moving in, I'd have an expanded marketing area for my paper route.

We moved to Laurel, Maryland, when I was twelve. As my parents found new places to shop, I discovered new possibilities for earning money. I got a job at the Cherry Brae Nursery, where Mom and Dad purchased shrubs and flowers. I watered flowers, planted seedling six-packs, and filled mum pots with dirt during the blazing summer heat. My kids groan when I recount this story of my first real job, punching the clock at Cherry Brae for two dollars and thirty-five cents an hour.

When Mom went to Mauck's Meat Market each month, I'd go along. The meat cutters fascinated me, probably because I'd heard my grandfather Harvey talk about his career as a meat-cutter. So, when I was in high school, I jumped at the chance for part-time work at Mauck's. There is an art to meat cutting, and I learned from the best. I mastered presenting the cut of meat on the butcher paper for customer approval before I weighed it, wrapped it, and wrote the price on the package. The job sharpened my math skills as I tallied prices on brown paper sacks when customers made multiple selections. A pencil behind the ear was a piece of the uniform, and on busy days, I'd sharpen it two or three times.

I loved cutting the meat, but my favorite part of the job was dealing with the public. I took pride in how I handled their selections, recommended a special cut, or shared secrets of cooking different cuts of meat. Often repeat customers would give up their place in line to wait for me to assist them. God was already preparing me for a career that used both my math and my people skills. Years later, I would handle people's investments with the same care and pride as I took with their meat purchases.

I enjoyed the job at Mauck's, but when the opportunity to work for my uncle's heating and air-conditioning business as a mechanic's helper came up that summer, I had a choice to make. At age seventeen, I left my full-time, six dollars an hour, summer meat-cutting job, for the construction job at ten dollars and fifty cents an hour. I did continue to work on Saturday's at Mauck's, since the construction was only Monday through Friday.

As I'd learned valuable retail skills as a meat-cutter, I learned the construction trade from my uncle. I learned about zoning and meeting codes at the same time that I learned how to dig trenches to lay pipes and wires under a foundation. I learned how to take inventory and clean the storage yards back at my uncle's office. After I proved myself knowledgeable and capable, my uncle promoted me to mechanic. The following summer I installed heat pumps in a new apartment complex. I had finished my first year in college, and I was so proud when my uncle assigned me a "company vehicle," an old 1966 Ford pick-up truck. Now *that* was a truck.

In 1979, following my sophomore year in college, I had the opportunity to spend the summer in Ocean City, Maryland with my friends. My meat-cutting skills came in handy, and the Super Fresh grocery store hired me at a great hourly wage. The only problem was that I had the graveyard shift, where I cut icy chickens from midnight until eight in the morning. After a week and a half, my fingers were numb from the cold and I was seeing chickens everywhere I looked!

The opportunity for a job as manager of the meat department at the 64th Street Market was the relief I needed from the chickens. I often opened and closed the market, assisted the general manager in ordering, and pitched in when other departments were short-handed. I worked long hours—I rarely saw the beach in the daylight—but the pay was great. At age nineteen, I was clearing five hundred dollars a week, enough to pay for tuition for a semester, my books, and some spending money.

Before I was out of my teens, I had worked my way through half a dozen occupations while maintaining excellent grades and lettering in football, baseball, and lacrosse. God not only gave me certain natural traits, but he also provided experiences that most people do not have until they enter the workforce as an adult. Gaining these skills as a sighted child and adolescent provided a foundation that supports me as a blind adult. I believe that God prepared me for my life of blindness.

***

In Matthew 25, Jesus tells the story of the three men who received talents (a measure of money) from their master before he left on a journey. When he returned, he found that two of the men invested their money and earned a return. The third man hid his money in the ground for fear that he might lose it. The master was pleased with the men who wisely invested their coins, but angry with the one that hid his. He took the money from this man and gave it to one who had invested wisely. My responsibility is to nurture the abilities and the experiences that God provides me. When I use them to live a successful and God-centered life today, I invest wisely in life.

I can achieve nothing on my own. Blind or sighted, only the love of Christ can make me whole. I would never trade who I have become as a blind child of God for any advantage another life might offer. I am committed to fulfilling God's plan for my life, using the talents he has given me, and relying on him in my weakness. After all, what if I find out that my sole mission on earth was to be a joyful witness to others through my blind condition? I don't want to stand before God one day and regret I missed my purpose in life. I am a sighted man in a blind body for now, but I know I have an eternity where my eyes will see, and I will be forever in God's presence.

19

Picking Up My Crosses Daily

If anyone would come after me, he must deny himself, pick up his cross daily and follow me.
Mathew 16:24

When I lost my sight, I knew that I had to face each day with a positive attitude and grow stronger in spite of my blindness. I didn't know many Bible verses at that time in my life, but it seemed that God placed the principles in my heart until I could discover his instruction in the scriptures.

One scripture that I did recall was that Jesus told his disciples that they must pick up their crosses daily and follow him. With the best of my understanding at the time, I accepted that blindness was one of my crosses. Jesus did not say that I have to like being blind, but that I have to accept it. In the Garden of Gethsemane, Jesus prayed to be spared from death on the cross (Matthew 26). But his prayer did not end there. Jesus prayed that the will of the Father, not his own, be done. And when God confirmed that the cross was the final step Jesus had to take, he accepted it. Our salvation came through the sacrificial love of Jesus on the cross. Jesus experienced complete isolation as he had his hands and feet nailed to the rough-hewn timbers. The Roman soldiers who pounded the nails through his flesh were among those that Jesus loved and came to save.

Jesus was both man and God. As man, he experienced all the fear and the pain of dying on the cross. As God, he chose to experience every emotional and physical condition of humankind. Thus, when Jesus told his disciples that they must take up their crosses daily and follow him, he did so with a full understanding of the physical and emotional burdens they would face. When Jesus says that I must take up the cross of blindness daily, he understands the full implication of that on every part of my life.

Jesus bore his cross, but it is humanly impossible for me to bear blindness on my own strength. Our Savior spoke to this human weakness as well. In the eleventh chapter of Matthew, Jesus says, "Come to me you who are weary and I will give you rest, for my burden is light and my yoke is easy." Jesus turns my cross into a yoke and he walks side-by-side with me in bearing the burden. When I share the load with Jesus, my burdens diminish as the yoke spreads out the weight.

***

My cross of blindness has both visible and invisible aspects. A person meeting me for the first time may not immediately realize that I cannot see. But soon they will notice the lack of eye contact, or my need of assistance from those around me. Blindness involves these tangible or visible constraints, but the greater struggle is usually internal. When I can't watch my daughter in the lead role of Clara, in *The Nutcracker*, my eyes swell with tears. I am denied the joy of watching her performance—and on a deeper level, denied the joy of ever seeing her beautiful face. And I experience anger that my daughter does not have a father who can see. The same emotions occur when my sons are involved in their activities. The burden of feeling cheated is so heavy sometimes it overwhelms me. When these emotions attack, ready to defeat me, I know that I have to give them to God to deal with. When I do, I remember the blessings that three loving children bring me every day. I may not be able to see their faces, but I rejoice in the sound of their voices, their hugs, and those special butterfly-kisses that my Tori Jean gives me every night before she goes to bed.

Another far-reaching aspect of the cross of blindness is the impact that it has on my wife. Stephanie willingly and lovingly chose to marry me, knowing that her part of the burden would be great. The load that she must carry to handle our family and household is enormous. This has become a cross that we both share, but from different perspectives. I wish that I could get the cars inspected, gassed up, and take care of things like obtaining the county stickers and license plates. I wish I could take the kids for a night out to give Stephanie a break. On a family camping trip, I'd like to make them feel more secure, knowing that I am there to protect them. I have to shoulder the cross of inferiority when I cannot mow the lawn, and maintain the mowers or other machinery. I do tackle many "Honey Do" tasks, like taking out the trash, cleaning the kitchen, fixing towel racks, washing the car, and switching storm windows and screens. But, the fact that we must hire more tradesmen than others not only costs more, but also requires that Stephanie be flexible enough to work around their schedules. It breaks my heart that I cannot take more chores away from her like reading mail, writing checks, or painting the children's rooms. Satan tries to get me to put myself down and accuses me of being worthless. I recognize his taunts, though, and I rejoice in performing those many tasks and duties that I am still able to contribute to our family.

***

As I wake each morning, I know that opening my eyes will not provide any information about my surroundings, and that realization is a new opportunity for Satan to plant seeds of frustration, fear, anger, or remorse over my condition—if I allow it. I can tell you that even after so many years of blindness, I must still declare war daily on desires to sink into bitterness, desperation, and depression. But God is faithful. Psalm 40 begins, "I waited patiently for the Lord to help me, and he turned to me and heard my cry. He lifted me out of the pit of despair, out of the mud and the mire" (NLT). When I lost my sight, God granted me not only the ability to forgive my assailant, but also the ability to shut out thoughts that drift towards remorse or resentment. Of course, I still get the blues occasionally, but God lifts me from the mire of self-pity. He helps me to reject the oppressive thoughts before they can take hold. It's as if I hardly need to evaluate the incoming threat before the Spirit and I react together. Actually, I think the Holy Spirit works on my behalf, slamming the doors on oppressive thoughts before they can bring me down.

Of course, I'd like to wake up with my sight restored. Jesus healed the blind and I know that he could heal me instantly, if that were the Father's will. Or he could restore my sight through technology, as new advances are made daily with artificial vision research. Someday, I may see again here on earth, but for now, I am blind. Like it or not, Stephanie and I both realize that our challenges are how it is, and we choose to move on. By accepting the cross of blindness and expressing gratitude for the life that we have, we gain strength in sharing both the burdens and the blessings.

20

Phantom Vision and Light Deprivation

I am the light of the world.
Whoever follows me will never walk in darkness,
but will have the light of life.
John 8:12

My wife says that I make blindness look too easy to the outside world. My day-to-day existence may appear effortless, but it is the result of a lot of unseen hard work and support—not just on my part, but also on that of my wife, children, co-workers, and friends.

When I speak about my blindness, my goals are to bring God glory, and to inspire others to make the best of whatever circumstances they are in. Life is like a game of cards, and you must play the hand you are dealt. I want a person to see that I live by my words: it is not what happened to me, but how I deal with it that matters. I talk of the victories I've experienced, and not about the hard work and pain that continue daily. No one likes a complainer, so I decided years ago that I wouldn't subject others to the difficult aspects of blindness. However, in this book I want to be completely transparent to show how God helps me to pick up and overcome hidden crosses day by day.

Just getting to work in the mornings is a production. I rely on my wife to match my clothing for me. I depend on the kids to put their book bags and sports equipment out of the way, so I don't trip over them while scurrying around to make coffee and get organized for leaving the house. Then, I depend on Stephanie to drive me to work.

At work, I might place my can of soda in the refrigerator upside-down to make it identifiable when I want it—only to have an unknowing person turn it right side up. I have that same perfectionist tendency, and I would have turned the can right side up, just like my co-workers, if I'd seen it upside-down. I have to educate them one at a time, that there is a method to my madness. At lunchtime, I can't hop in the car and drive to get Chinese food or run an errand, so I brown-bag it a lot. However, these daily inconveniences are minor skirmishes compared to the ongoing battle I face with phantom vision and the effects of light deprivation.

***

My field of vision went black the instant that I was shot in 1980. About two months later, this dark field became speckled with phantom pinpricks of white or yellow light. These "stars," as I call them, were few enough that I could count them when they occurred. They caught my attention as they danced around in my old upper right visual field.

Dramatic visual hallucinations soon replaced the stars, as realistic as though my sight had returned. The first series of these visions reminded me of intricate Oriental pen-and-ink art. Dragons and serpents moved about in the foreground while beautiful waterfalls and flower designs were in the distance. Most of the figures were muted greens, blues, grays, and yellows, highlighted by touches of white. Within a few days, the Oriental visions changed to a jungle scene. In particular, a giraffe would regularly pop into my old visual field. The giraffe and other jungle animals moved along in a row, their heads and upper bodies showing above brilliant green vegetation.

Rows of stacked yellow blocks trimmed in blue or green eventually replaced the animals. The blocks seemed to be on conveyer belts—some stacks moved vertically and others moved horizontally. Each stack was on a different plane, constantly moving but never colliding. I thought this was crazy stuff, but then I decided to consider it entertainment.

Years later, I learned that these visual hallucinations are common phenomena when a sighted person suddenly loses his sight. In the late 1700s, a Swiss philosopher, Charles Bonnet first described this syndrome, which now bears his name. Usually Charles Bonnet Syndrome hallucinations go away after a few months. Over time, the vivid figures and moving blocks faded into seas of white, yellow, and gray stars that swirled into changing patterns and filled my old visual field.

After all these years, I continue to "see" these phantom stars. These pinpricks of light remind me of a snowy television screen when tuned to a channel that is not broadcasting. Some days, the stars are calm and move about gently. Other days they flash violently. They alternate every other day on approximately sixteen to thirty-hour cycles. I call these "good star days" and "bad star days."

I am able to ignore the snowy field and concentrate on my work on the good star days. Sometimes the calm stars appear to group together, creating a virtual image of objects that I touch.

On what I refer to as the bad star days, the snowy screen explodes like fireworks, with flashing and darting stars that demand my attention and drain me of energy. Concentrating on my work is difficult and sometimes impossible on these turbulent-star days. As I speak to clients on the phone, make stock trades, or do market research, I am constantly battling the distraction and resultant stress of the stars flashing in my face. On extreme days, the distraction makes it nearly impossible to read Braille.

The calm and turbulent days are cyclical. I underwent testing at the National Institutes of Health with a doctor who was a world authority in the field of light deprivation and stimulation. He attempted to find a correlation between my stars and my circadian rhythm—the energy cycle we all undergo as adults. Despite copious notes, he could not determine specific patterns or suggest anything to diminish the bad star days.

So, I continue to deal with these turbulent days by asking God to strengthen me, and then I move forward. Sometimes I feel like I'm grinding my way ahead into a sandstorm of stars, but I try never to give up. It would often be much easier to take a nap than deal with the stars, but I will only prosper by putting my shoulder to the grindstone. I think about the sacrifice and pain Jesus suffered to give me eternal life, and my stars don't seem so bad. I continue working and praying through the distraction, but the energy expended on turbulent-star days leaves me stressed and exhausted.

***

The other debilitating result of my blindness is light deprivation. Light deprivation affects even sighted people, who may suffer from seasonal affective disorder with symptoms of sadness, depression, and difficulty sleeping during the shortened days of winter. During war times, prisoners were tortured by placing them in dark cells for days, weeks, or months. Studies on light deprivation show that the participants soon lose track of day and night, and find it difficult to concentrate or stay awake for any length of time, even when they have slept eight or nine hours.

Our biological clocks are set and are dependent on light and darkness. The brain secretes melatonin when we first perceive daylight with our eyes. This hormone helps to regulate sleeping and waking patterns. God planned this perfect system when he separated the day from the night, and created man to need regular cycles of rest.

Without sight, my body does not know when to produce melatonin and initiate the regular cycle. My days normally run between sixteen- and thirty-hour cycles, causing a biological clock that "slides" fifteen to thirty minutes a day. This sliding biological clock produces an eight thirty a.m. to ten p.m. wake/sleep cycle one day; a few days later my body wants to wake at nine a.m. and fall asleep closer to midnight. This cycle continues causing me to have sleepless nights followed by days of exhaustion.

When my clock is operating in a normal range, my calm star days seem to increase. When my clock is off schedule, I must deal with the double affliction of sleep deprivation and the flashing stars exploding in my visual field.

***

I know that God spared my life in 1980. I prayed that if I lived, I would deal with being blind. Over the years, I've continued to thank God for letting me live. I've accepted the inconveniences of being blind, but the torture that comes from the lack of sleep and the turbulent-star days was not in my concept of blindness.

Why doesn't God answer my prayers and take this mental pain away? I don't know, but I do know that he helps me bear the pain when I go to him in prayer. Sometimes a special verse of scripture will come to my mind, or I'll remember that Jesus has prepared a place for me in heaven—and there will be no pain or sorrow there. Praying through the distractions on turbulent-star days is my only comfort.

I compare my struggle with phantom vision and light deprivation to Biblical accounts of Job and Paul. In the Old Testament, God allowed Satan to heap pain and troubles on Job, including taking his wealth, killing his children, and covering him with painful sores. Through all of his suffering, Job's friends contended that he had sinned. Job denied that he had any secret sin, and then in his pain, he questioned God's fairness in allowing him to suffer. God answered Job by reminding him that he was the creator of the world and everything in it. Job didn't have to think the suffering was fair; he only needed to remember that God was in control.

In the New Testament, Paul writes of a thorn in his flesh. In Second Corinthians 12:7-8, he says, "to keep me from becoming conceited because of these surpassingly great revelations, there was given me a thorn in my flesh, a messenger of Satan to torment me. Three times I pleaded with the Lord to take it away from me." Many scholars think that Paul had a chronic physical affliction to deal with daily. Paul begged God to remove the affliction, but when God did not, Paul accepted it, and continued with his ministry.

***

I've begged God to spare me the ongoing pain of phantom vision and light deprivation. I even tried acupuncture treatments along with my prayers, but nothing has removed these afflictions. These are certainly thorns in my flesh, and part of the cross of blindness that Jesus has called me to bear as I follow him. I could never compare my stress to the agony Jesus faced on the cross, but I find comfort knowing that Jesus prayed for relief, even when his ultimate decision was for the Father's will to be done. As Jesus prayed, I have also learned to pray—*Father, strengthen me to accept your will, so I might carry it out for your glory.*

21

Joy in All Circumstances

Consider it pure joy, my brothers, whenever you face trials of many kinds, because you know that the testing of your faith develops perseverance. Perseverance must finish its work so that you may be mature and complete, not lacking anything.
James 1:2-4

One of my axioms in life is *squeeze the joy out of every day before the day squeezes the joy out of you*! I have to admit that some days, I feel like I'm in a squeezing match with the devil. For every drop of joy I can muster up, he tightens the screws trying to get two drops of frustration. Sunday mornings are a typical squeezing match for many Christian families, including mine. I'm dressed, ready to go to church—but one of the boys is on the computer, or my daughter is still deciding on what to wear. I flip the crystal and touch the face of my watch—we're going to be late... again. I feel frustration and anger building up inside of me. Does that sound familiar?

I learned years ago that my morning attitude is the baseline for the rest of my day. I must still deal with the hurdles before me—physical, mental, and emotional ones—both at work and with my family. If I choose anger or frustration, not only will I be miserable throughout the day, but my misery also spreads to those around me. If I decide to face the day with joy, the same thing happens: my joy spreads to my family and my co-workers.

***

You've probably seen all those bumper stickers over the years: Happiness is Having Grandchildren, Happiness is a Pekinese, and Happiness is Retirement. On and on they go. Although joy and happiness are related, they are not the same thing. I can be unhappy that my family is dawdling on Sunday morning, and still choose joy. I can be unhappy with situations beyond my control, and still choose joy. I can be unhappy that I have to expend so much more energy than a sighted person does, just to get through the day, but I can still choose joy.

Joy is the natural result of an attitude of gratitude. No matter what my circumstances, I know that I am blessed. I need to look no further than a new day dawning to find joy. According to God's will, the earth keeps spinning and the sun continues to rise and set on schedule. As the psalmist says, "Where every morning dawns and every evening fades, you call forth songs of joy" (Psalm 68:8b).

I recall walking the beach one night when I was ten or eleven, and marveling at the glistening trail that the moon made across the sea. The beauty of the sight was so gripping I wanted to share it with someone. Perhaps you've run inside and called for your family to come and see a beautiful rainbow after a summer storm, or a constellation on a starry night. How much more God wants to call to us: *Come share my joy in creation! Breathe in the beauty, and breathe out expressions of joy.*

Sure, God could share his masterpieces with the angels in heaven, but the Father's heart offers a relationship to humanity. His desire is that we seek him first, every day, and that we share his joy throughout the day. Having an attitude of gratitude and pausing throughout the day to thank God for my blessings allows me to tap into his joy. Asking him for guidance as the day's events unfold also permits me to see God at work in my life.

***

When I get up in the morning, I focus on the things that I can do rather than those I can't. I remember an old saying,

"I was resentful that I had no shoes, and then I met a beggar who had no feet." Although I live a comfortable life, I know that spiritually I am just a beggar who has found some bread. But one day I will sit at the banquet table of the King. The thought of that truth helps me face each day with humbleness and gratitude. When I pray the way Jesus modeled in the Lord's Prayer, I know that God will provide for my every need. "Give us this day our daily bread" instills a solid foundation for living the day with joy. My joy comes from knowing that the things I truly need always have been, and always will be, provided. Faith and fear cannot co-exist, so I choose to live by faith and do not fear anything that the day brings forth.

I am a human, though. And even with the best intentions, it can be hard to stay in the spiritual groove. Challenges come at me every hour of the day. Even worse, when things are going well, I find myself drifting away and interrupting the rhythm of my daily quiet prayer life. When I am not moving towards God, I am moving away from him. And when that happens, I deprive myself of his affection and wisdom. I also don't allow him the joy of being my intimate provider and helper when I stop counting on him.

***

Worrying about the cares of the world is one of the greatest joy robbers I know. Cares are like idols—things that demand our attention, rather than our attention being focused on God. In 2002, my faith and my ability to keep my attention on God were buffeted as the country faced a failing stock market.

The bear market started in 2000 and continued through the first quarter of 2003, and the start of war in Iraq. Not only was it a difficult time emotionally, but the situation also threatened the financial stability of my clients and my own investments. By July of 2002, the S&P had lost half of its value. Every investor was trying to second-guess the market. People were in a panic. Anxious and angry people bombarded me all day long. In the evenings, I would sit alone in the kitchen. I was so burned out that I could not even speak to my family, or engage them in any meaningful way.

I even found myself wondering what else a blind person could do to earn a comparable living. One day, I realized that I was as stressed as my clients were—I'd bought a new home seven months previously and my old one had not sold, and that financial burden was weighing heavily on me. This was a turning point: I could totally stress out, or I could trust in the Lord. I began spending more and more time in the word and discovered that I couldn't isolate myself in worry and depression over things beyond my control. I believed that God cared about me, and I had to trust him to take care of me as his child.

It was during this stormy period that I realized my calling was higher than only buying and selling securities. I had the opportunity to be a beacon in the waves—an opportunity that I was only able to accept through the calming strength of the Holy Spirit. Panicked clients began to comment, "I know you don't control the markets, but I sure feel better after talking to you." I don't think I am a particularly wise person, but when I approached each day with my priorities right, God was able to use me and provided the words that others needed to hear. And, I discovered that when I started my day in prayer, the Holy Spirit would fill me with a peace and joy that took me through the day.

Of course, not every client appreciated my positive attitude during the bear market. Many times the conversations were (and sometimes still are) most challenging when I answered the phone with a joyful attitude and the client snapped, "How can you be so happy in this mess? Of course, what do you brokers care, you make money whether we buy or sell, so it doesn't matter to you if we lose money."

When I relied on God's strength, I did not react defensively to their aggression. Proverbs 29:11 says, "A fool gives full vent to his anger, but a wise man keeps himself under control." I had to rise above their fear and greed and provide a perspective that would calm them down. But during the worst of the market declines, even my joy came under attack with all of the conflict around me. When that happened, I'd take a break and escape to the quiet of the men's room to pray. "Father," I'd call out, "give me the words to say. Give me contagious joy and let others see your peace in me during this chaos." Maintaining a Christian demeanor takes work in the heat of battle. So throughout the day, I would remind myself that JOY can stand for "Jesus Over You." When all around me was caving in, I was only able to stand because I knew the Lord was the source of my joy.

Proverbs 12: 18 says, "Reckless words pierce like a sword, but the tongue of the wise brings healing." I wanted my clients and friends to see gentleness in my reactions to even their aggressive outbursts. Through gentleness, I was able to let the joy of the Lord shine through during a dark valley of my career.

22

The Fairness Trap

*Here's another old saying that
deserves a second look:
"Eye for eye, tooth for tooth."
Is that going to get us anywhere?
Here's what I propose:
"Don't hit back at all."
If someone strikes you, stand there and take it.
If someone drags you into court and sues for the
shirt off your back, gift wrap your best coat
and make a present of it.
And if someone takes unfair advantage of you,
use the occasion to practice the servant life.
No more tit-for-tat stuff. Live generously.
Matthew 5:38-42 The Message*

Desiring fairness is part of man's nature, but fairness is not one of the basics of life promised by God. Instead,

God promises to provide us with the strength to find victory in our circumstances.

Satan often uses the lure of unfairness to trap us. Was it fair that God forbade Adam and Eve to eat from the tree of life (Genesis 2:17)? Was God keeping something good from them? Or, in the story of Joseph (Genesis 37), was it fair that his father, Jacob, favored him over his other sons? What happens when a person acts on perceived unfair treatment? Because Adam and Eve ate of the fruit, they were expelled from the garden God had prepared for them. Joseph's brothers sold him into slavery, and although they were later reunited and forgiven, they lived with the burden of guilt.

When acquaintances hear my story, they often say it was unfair that I had to spend a lifetime without sight because of the actions of another person. Then the conversation comes around to the question—what happened to the young man who shot me? Go with me back to 1980, to my assailant's trial, and see how God taught me about "the fairness trap."

***

December 1980. Hagerstown Circuit Court. Mom, Dad, and I sat erect and motionless as Judge Wright called my assailant forward and then read the charges aloud: *Assault with a deadly weapon.* Was that all? The judge didn't even mention battery, or the fact that my entire future was changed.

"Young man, do you understand these charges brought against you?"

"Yes, your honor." That was the first time I heard the voice of the man who had taken my sight and changed my life. I tried to picture him: how tall he was, if he looked like a scoundrel, if he looked sorry for what he'd done. He stood just a matter of feet away from where we sat, but I couldn't tell too much because his voice was faint and sounded either dejected or unconcerned.

"What is your plea?"

"Guilty, your honor."

I took a deep breath. At least the fellow had admitted his crime.

What happened next seemed like a cheesy TV drama where the lawyers and judge worked out a plea bargain in advance. Judge Wright sentenced the man who permanently took away my sight to three years in jail. Before I had time to reflect on the brevity of this sentence, the judge continued. "However, because of the overcrowding in the local jails, I am suspending the entire sentence. You will be on probation for the three-year period, and you will perform thirty hours of community service." Then he boomed, "Do you understand that if you violate your parole even once, that three-year sentence will begin immediately?"

I nearly choked. This dude was getting off with thirty hours of community service, yet I was sentenced to a lifetime of darkness. I was outraged and insulted. Who had just been incarcerated?

We left the courtroom in shock. Once we were outside, Dad told me that my assailant had appeared with a fresh haircut and a new suit, giving an appearance of the nice boy next door. The convoluted thought came to me that maybe I should have worn dark glasses and come in with my cane. Maybe I should have looked more like a blind man. Did the judge glance at me and think I didn't look like I had suffered from the assault?

I should have been voicing my outrage and my parents should have been crying in defeat, but we just stood there. We were truly shell-shocked, stunned, and incapable of responding. The District Attorney surfaced from the crowd and apologized that there was no jail time for the assailant. I don't remember what response we offered. We were so astonished that I don't think we said a thing.

As the attorney walked away—back into his nice sighted life and on to the next client—I wanted to erupt. I wanted to yell at someone. Anyone! For a split second, I debated whether to go after my assailant or the judge.

The same feelings of anger that I'd tried to muster up on the front porch in Sharpsburg slammed against me again. By anyone's measure, I was the one who received the short end of the stick—and it felt like I was being beaten by the long end of it.

I'd surrendered to God once that day on the porch. I felt no malice for this young man, but I still thought he would receive a consequence for his actions. I grew up thinking the legal system protected the victim and provided penalties for the criminals. I was angry at the situation and angry with the judge. The whole situation was unfair. What was my assailant to learn from his day in court? It's okay to break the law, even if it affects other's lives? It's okay, because you only have to serve thirty hours of community service? I worked more than thirty hours a week in my summer jobs. This guy was getting off with less than one week's work. Perhaps if he'd had to walk in a blind man's shoes for thirty hours, I'd have been satisfied with the sentence, but picking up trash? Or working in a soup kitchen? Maybe my anger on the porch a few months earlier was wrong, but this time I had every right to be angry.

Or did I? What was I thinking? God had already given me complete peace that he was in charge. My blindness would not improve if my assailant were properly chastised and punished. Whatever happened to him did not change one thing for me. To move forward with my recovery, I had to turn the issue of fairness over to God. Yet, having to live without sight seemed to be a harsh requirement for me, and completely unfair.

***

Actually, I faced two issues of fairness. First, was it fair that I lost my sight? Second, was it fair that my assailant got off practically free since the jails were overcrowded? When Judge Wright handed down the suspended sentence, the fairness snare was set before me. My family felt that justice was indeed blind, and not in the sense of lack of favoritism, but in the sense of ignoring victim's rights. I was blind for life. Having my assailant serve time was not going to change anything for me, but the fact that he got off with such a light sentence seemed unfair in the eyes of the world.

I could have easily settled into the fairness trap. I did question God, but my question was "why" not "why me?" I didn't consider myself any more or less worthy of having a tragedy strike me as the next person. I didn't question why the bullet came through my house and not the one next door. I did question why the situation had to happen at all. I didn't get an answer to the "why," but as God held a mirror before my rage on the front porch, he replaced the questioning with a peace that knowing why wouldn't change anything.

I could let go of my questioning and move forward toward emotional healing, or fall into the fairness trap and allow resentment to harden my heart. I had to choose between becoming bitter or becoming better. I remember thinking that this was a way of turning the other cheek, instead of swinging back in revenge. I have to admit that it didn't seem fair (see, there's the trap lurking again), but if Jesus said to turn the other cheek, then that was what I needed to do.

Resentment would have turned into anger and that would have turned back on me, destroying my life. My cynical disposition would have had harmful effects on every life I touched, and especially those who loved me.

***

In late fall of 1983, a few weeks before my assailant was to complete his three-year probationary period, he struck again. This time he shot and wounded his girlfriend; then he killed himself. I was stunned when I heard the news. The thought came to me that the real unfairness of the suspended sentence was to my assailant, not to me. If he had been jailed, and received counseling, would he be starting his life of freedom with a changed heart? Perhaps I would have had the opportunity to tell him that I forgave him. Perhaps I could have told him about the Savior, the one who suffered the ultimate act of unfairness; the one who taught me to forgive.

23

Eternity Bound

There is a river whose streams make glad the city of God; the holy place where the Most High dwells.
Psalm 46:4

Nothing excites or delights me more than thinking about heaven. My mind creates scenes that dazzle me with the joyous moment when I will receive new sight that lasts forever! As a Christian, I am already a citizen of the Kingdom of God, and someday, I'll take up residence in that holy place where the Most High lives. For the time being, though, my home is here on earth. And while I am here, God wants a relationship with me that will sustain me in every way. Jesus called that sustaining relationship "abiding," when he spoke to his disciples before his death on the cross:

I am the true vine, and My Father is the vinedresser. Every branch in Me that does not bear fruit He takes away; and every branch that bears fruit He prunes, that it may bear more fruit. You are already clean because of the word which I have spoken to you. Abide in Me, and I in you. As the branch cannot bear fruit of itself, unless it abides in the vine, neither can you, unless you abide in Me.

I am the vine, you are the branches. He who abides in Me, and I in him, bears much fruit; for without Me you can do nothing. If anyone does not abide in Me, he is cast out as a branch and is withered; and they gather them and throw them into the fire, and they are burned. If you abide in Me, and My words abide in you, you will ask what you desire, and it shall be done for you. By this My Father is glorified, that you bear much fruit; so you will be My disciples.

As the Father loved Me, I also have loved you; abide in My love. If you keep My commandments, you will abide in My love, just as I have kept My Father's commandments and abide in His love. These things I have spoken to you, that My joy may remain in you, and that your joy may be full. This is My commandment, that you love one another as I have loved you. John 15:1-12 NKJV

Andrew Murray takes readers on a thirty-one day journey through these twelve verses in his classic, *Abide in Christ* (Whitaker House, 1979). In the book preface, he writes:

During the life of Jesus on earth, the word he chiefly used when speaking of the relationship of the disciples to Himself was, "Follow me" (Matthew 4:19). When about to leave for heaven, He gave them a new word, in which their more intimate and spiritual union with Him in glory would be expressed. That chosen word was "Abide in Me" (John 15:4).

Murray was only one of many respected theologians who wrote about the mystery of abiding in Christ, as referred to in the book of John. I am not a theologian, and I know that my human understanding is limited, but every day I try to learn more about what it means to abide in Christ.

To me, abiding is not a passive state but a continuous pursuit of a relationship with God. In 1 Corinthians 9, Paul speaks of athletes being in training to win a crown that will not last, but Christians are in training for the crown that will last forever—eternal life in heaven with Christ. I like to think of abiding as growing closer to Christ, with the Holy Spirit as my trainer. My spiritual training regime involves exercises of all sorts. I need to exercise my faith to cheerfully face another day of blind life and rise above the fray. It is important to exercise justice and good judgment based on the wisdom I gather from the written word and learning from past mistakes. My journey tends to feel less bumpy when I exercise my ability to pray, talk, and listen to God.

***

I hunger for God's word, and find that like regular physical exercise, I need to read and meditate on the word daily. Job 22:22 says, "Accept instruction from his mouth and lay up his words in your heart." Without sight, I primarily rely on learning the word by hearing. My mind translates the auditory signals into *written* words on my mental slate, and stores them in my heart. During times of joy, and particularly during times of stress, the Holy Spirit reminds me of the scripture I need.

My granddad Harvey used to say, "Any day your feet hit the floor is a good day." He appreciated every day of life that he lived. I agree with his saying, but I simply add, "Any day your feet *and your knees* hit the floor is a good day."

As part of my spiritual training, I begin each day by communing with God in prayer. I praise him and thank him for who he is, for being in control of the universe and caring enough to be in control of my life, and for simply choosing to sustain me another day here on earth. I thank Jesus for dying on the cross for my salvation and for giving me a clean slate each day. I ask God to fill me with his Holy Spirit and I ask for wisdom and guidance, so that he might be glorified by the fruit my branch produces. I express my gratitude for all of the blessings that God has given me. Then I ask God's forgiveness for any trespasses and seek his help in tackling my shortcomings.

I have to be careful not to slip into simply thinking about and planning for my day under the guise of prayer. When that happens, I apologize to God and try again. I want my time with him to be dynamic and interactive, not a recitation of the same words every morning. I desire to stay in communion with him throughout the day; however, as circumstances and challenges occur, I sometimes forget to turn to him for guidance. That is why it is called spiritual training, or practice, to develop the habit of turning to the throne of grace for guidance. There is certainly nothing automatic about it. When I do seek God's presence, the privilege of seeing him work around and through me is a special blessing.

On those days I try to do things on my own, and do not place myself fully in his control, I am in danger of reckless abandonment of my faith. God lets me take control, but when I do, I am powerless. I compare this to a water skier who falls but continues to hold onto the rope to maintain control of the situation. Instead of control, this situation results in a wave bashing. Relief only comes when the skier lets go, and rests in his or her lifejacket, floating in the comfortable waters until picked up. God wants me to let go and lean on him for everything I need. He is my Lifejacket. When I let go, God's Spirit leads me safely through even choppy waters.

***

I'll continue my training to abide in my Lord and Savior until the day that I go home to heaven. Living each day with joy and satisfaction allows me to focus on those things that are unseen by physical eyes, as Paul wrote in 2 Corinthians 4:17-18, "For our light and momentary troubles are achieving for us an eternal glory that far outweighs them all. So we fix our eyes not on what is seen, but on what is unseen. For what is seen is temporary, but what is unseen is eternal."

Not long ago, I was invited to share my story with the teen group at church. On the evening of the event, I waited with a friend in a room adjacent to the youth meeting. The kids' happy chatter filled the building as they snacked on cookies and punch. Then the youth director called for their attention. "Okay everyone; we are doing something different tonight. I have bandanas for all of you, take one, and tie it around your head as a blindfold." Inquisitive banter replaced the earlier chatter, but in a few minutes there was silence, and I assumed they had complied with the instruction. The director spoke again, "The other leaders and I will lead you into the next room where you will need to sit quietly until we start. Do not remove the blindfolds until you are told to do so."

Shuffling feet entered the meeting room as the beautiful words to a praise song about Jesus taking the nails and the thorns for our sins filled the air. At that moment, the Holy

Spirit inspired me. "Can you get a blindfold for me, also?" I whispered to the friend standing with me.

He retrieved a bandana, which I tied over my eyes. Then he whispered, "You're on." and led me to the front of the room.

***

"Good evening, ladies and gentlemen! My name is Chris Harvey, and for the next few minutes, I'd like you to experience my world. You see, I am blind…"

I proceeded to share how I lost my sight, and told of the blessings God provided in the process. At the end of my chat, I instructed the kids to remove their blindfolds. As they did, they saw me standing before them with an identical bandana covering my eyes.

"Praise God that your blindfold came off and you can see again. My blindfold will not come off until I arrive in heaven, where I will be able to see forever." I continued speaking with my blindfold on. "But, that is alright by me. My time on earth without sight is brief in relationship to eternity, so I choose to stay focused on what God wants to do through me while I am here. Think about your own gifts and talents and how you fit into the lives of others. Use your gifts and relationships to God's glory, and you will be a blessing to the people you encounter. Your life can be a reflection of Christ to those who do not yet know him. I am grateful for the worst thing that has ever happened in my life, because God has used it to his glory—and he will work all of the things that happen in your life to his glory, when you count on him."

The youth director later told me that many of the kids had tears in their eyes as I spoke. I never intend for my story to be a tearjerker, because the real story is one of victory. But sometimes the Holy Spirit uses tears as he draws us closer to our Savior.

***

Most people cannot imagine good coming from being shot and blinded. As an optimist, I look at my blind condition as a way to reach others for God. I believe I have been a better witness without sight than I might have been if I could see. I wish I did not stand out—but a blind person does; so, I choose to use this spotlight to point to God and his desire to bring good out of all circumstances, for in him there is victory.

My story does not end with the victory here on earth, though. The end of my story is eternal—eternal sighted life in heaven. I rejoice knowing that the face of Jesus Christ, my Savior, will be the first thing I will behold with restored vision. I delight in knowing that I'll also see the faces of my beautiful wife and my precious children for the first time.

I'll celebrate with other family and friends in the City of God, where there are no imperfections in any of us, and there is neither pain nor sorrow. And when I'm introduced to the other believers in heaven, I think I'll say, "So, I used to be a blind guy on earth. What were you?"

Acknowledgments

Rest assured that you would not be reading this book if it were not for Vie Herlocker. Her writing talent, resources, guidance, and dedication to this project have been invaluable to me.

As I closed in on the final manuscript, I also valued the editing services of Michelle Levigne.

To my friend, Lt. Col. Oliver North, thank you for your advice and encouragement with my project.

A special thanks to Chuck Graves, who faithfully built and still maintains my website, www.visionwithoutsight.net.

My many thanks go to Stephanie, Craig, and Charlotte for contributing chapters to the book. Their recollections added a unique dimension to my story.

Thank you to David Brown. We met as broker trainees in 1983 and he has become one of my best friends, not just for reading chart patterns for me, but also for his brotherhood, as we have endured many harsh market cycles together.

I also appreciate the Christian upbringing my parents provided for me. They set the example, and Stephanie and I are continuing the tradition by raising our children on the foundation of the Holy Word.

For the last five years, I have benefited from the wisdom found in my Monday night Men's Accountability Group, so I sure appreciate my brothers Jan, Dick, Butch, and Jim for their reliable support and sage advice.

I would like to acknowledge Dr. Alan Stanford, Dr. Chris Walker, and Pastor Gary Hamrick for their contributions to my spiritual growth, mentoring me both from the pulpit and one-on-one as friends.

Finally, thank you, Father God. You started a great work in me, and you will be faithful to complete it in the day of our Lord Jesus Christ.

Note from the Author

So this is it. This is where I end the book others asked me to write, and the Holy Spirit placed on my heart. I feel privileged to leave this memoir to my readers, friends, family, and especially to my children. I hope that my words will help them to understand my sincere effort to handle my blindness as best as I can, and how much my walk with Jesus means to me. And to assure them that they should rejoice when I pass on, because I will not pass away. When I cross over to the heavenly realm, I will simultaneously kneel down, dance before, jump toward, shout praises to, and hug Jesus! I often say, "The thunder you will hear at my funeral will be me dancing and looking around a whole lot in heaven."

Meanwhile, I'll rejoice in my blind condition here on earth. I'll go on putting my index finger in the coffee cup or water glass to know when it is full, and move my hand towards lamps to feel the heat to know if they are on or off, until the day I die. Reading bumps will be second nature until then, as will listening to talking computers instead of viewing the information that I need. Each morning, I will rise and try to sort out what kind of a phantom vision or star day it will be, while others simply need to check the weather. I will continue adapting customs and techniques to deal with not being able to see, and carrying on as a warrior in the spiritual battlefield of life.

I hope this book has blessed you in some way, because it sure has blessed me working on it. The project was a labor of love and provided many hours of soul searching. It has forced me to take a closer look at the blind creature I am, and more importantly, it has brought me into a closer relationship with God.

So, until we meet in heaven, remember to squeeze the joy out of every day, before the day squeezes the joy out of you, and to God be the Glory!

Chris

Printed in the United States
206550BV00002B/154-1194/P